MY LIFE
AT APPLE

MY LIFE

AT APPLE

(AND THE STEVE I KNEW)

John Couch
WITH JASON TOWNE

Waterside Productions
Cardiff-by-the-Sea, CA

Printed in the United States of America

First Printing, 2021

ISBN-13: 978-1-951805-84-5 print edition
ISBN-13: 978-1-951805-85-2 ebook edition

Waterside Productions
2055 Oxford Ave
Cardiff, CA 92007
www.waterside.com

For Steve

AUTHOR'S NOTE

This memoir covers events that took place in my life that led to my becoming Apple Computer's 54th employee, my decades-long tenure as an Apple executive and Vice President, and the relationship I had with Apple co-founder Steve Jobs, both as my boss and my friend. This book is not intended to be a biography of Steve Jobs nor an official historical account of Apple. All names, dates, events, quotes, and other information are accurate to the best of my knowledge. However, I did need to rely on memory when primary sources were no longer available and because of this dialogue may at times be paraphrased. Throughout the book I describe various aspects of Steve which include his behaviors, traits, characteristics, and motivations, but these are based on my own personal perspective, interpretation, and experiences. In other words, this memoir is specifically about *my* life at Apple and the Steve *I* knew, which will be very different from the Steve you knew or knew about.

CONTENTS

FOREWORD

My Life at Apple and the Steve I Knew paints a mesmerizing picture of the extraordinary life of my former Apple colleague, college alumnus, and long-time friend, John Couch. Over forty years ago Steve Jobs introduced me to John, already a brilliant, seasoned software engineer at a time when very few existed. Like me, John had graduated from UC Berkeley, becoming one of the first computer science graduates in the country. Also like me, he went on to work under the leadership of Bill Hewlett, Hewlett-Packard's visionary CEO and co-founder.

Given such a strong (and familiar) pedigree, I wasn't surprised to learn that Steve had shown up on John's doorstep with an Apple II as a gift, intent on recruiting him to help Apple develop a new, revolutionary computer that would change the world. Steve was his usual persuasive self and, like me, John became one of Apple's earliest employees. He would go on to become Apple's first Director of New Products, first Vice President of Software, one of its first General Managers and, years later, its first Vice President of Education. Most importantly, John would become one of Apple's most valuable and influential people, even though you may not have heard of him, until now.

You might consider this book a historical journey, filled with never-before-told stories about Apple, Steve, John, and their decades-long relationship. If you think you've heard all there is to hear about the ins and outs of early Apple and the complexities of Steve Jobs, you are mistaken. Even with dozens of books written and movies made about Apple and Steve, few have been told in such a personal way as you will read here. Even stories you've heard a million times become fresh when told from John's unique point of view. He is a master storyteller, capable of making you feel as though you were right there in the room with him, seeing what he saw and hearing what he heard, during some of the most pivotal moments in Apple's history, like his visit to Xerox PARC with Steve to see the Alto Computer, Mike Scott's infamous Black Wednesday firings, Apple's IPO, and launch day for three different computers.

One of my favorite stories in the book came during John's first week at Apple when he and Steve met with a third-party vendor in a conference room. Steve, fashionably late, walks in barefoot, sits cross-legged in the middle of the conference table, and after inspecting the vendor's printer for about 30 seconds declares, "This is a piece of shit," and then walks back out. Other stories I love include the time John and Steve tried to recruit John Sculley to leave Pepsi to become Apple's CEO, the time John found a certificate for 7.5 million Apple shares lying in Steve's front yard, and a deeply moving conversation that John and Steve had on an airplane in the midst of an active bomb threat. Steve once told John that he was one of the most trustworthy individuals he knew and publicly toasted him for their twenty-plus years of friendship, so it's no surprise that John has so many personal moments to share.

While this book does a great job of capturing Steve's human side, I was just as impressed to read about how John was able to lead his team to create one of the most revolutionary computers in history—Lisa. Referred to in the media as "The Father of Lisa," John oversaw the entire Lisa program, designing and developing the game-changing advancement of what we refer to as *Lisa Technology*. I get particularly frustrated when I hear people describe Lisa as an Apple failure, because they don't realize how much of a success it actually was, not just for

Apple, but for the entire computer industry. It was John who conceived of, and wrote a paper on, a concept he called "datagramming" that set the strategic direction for Apple software and drastically influenced the design and development of the graphical-user interface (GUI) used in both Lisa and Macintosh.

Because of datagramming, Lisa was able to introduce mainstream markets to a GUI that included things we now take for granted like a Windows-based operating system, a computer "desktop," icons, files, folders, and menu bars, as well as our ability to copy, paste, edit, drag, drop, save and retrieve documents. John and his Lisa team also designed and introduced the world to things such as the modern-day mouse, digital rights management (DRM), and bundled office software suites. All of these were crucial developments and one of the main reasons non-programmers can easily use computers today.

The truth is that Lisa was the most revolutionary computer the world had ever seen. While Macintosh gets most of the credit, if it had not been for the innovations that John introduced with Lisa, there may not have been a Macintosh. On that note, in one of the most memorable stories in this book, John tells of the time Bill Gates picked him and his young son, Kris, up from the airport, gave them a personal tour of Microsoft's campus, and ended the day with Bill saying to Kris, "You'll never know the impact your dad had on Microsoft and the computer industry." It was true, because without John's *Lisa Technology* there may have been no Microsoft Windows or Microsoft Office either. Lisa forever changed the way computers were designed and used and reshaped an entire industry in its image.

Perhaps the most impressive thing for me was, even after all that, John was just getting started. After Lisa's release, he left Apple to explore new opportunities. He became an angel investor, a corporate adviser, led the transformation of a K-12 school, and was CEO of a genomics startup whose work on mapping the human genome paved the way for today's companies like 23andMe and Ancestory.com. After Steve returned to Apple he reached back out to John, asking him to join him again, this time as Apple's first Vice President of Education, now tasked with using his leadership and creative talents to transform its struggling education business. This time around John oversaw the design of a technology-driven pedagogy called Challenge Based Learning, as well as a host of influential products and programs like iTunes U (which led to MOOCs), School Nights (which led to Apple Camps), and a university-based app development program that has now gone global. Incredibly, in just ten years, John grew Apple's education business from $1 billion to more than $9 billion, with his work once again influencing an entire industry.

Over the years, my wife Janet and I continue to be close friends with John. He is one of the most interesting, intelligent, and passionate people I've ever met. Both Steve and I viewed him as an essential part of what made Apple the most innovative company in the world, even as he remained one of our best-kept secrets. But now the secret is out. For the first time ever, John is sharing his story publicly, giving the rest of the world an opportunity to appreciate his relationship with Steve and with myself. I promise that when you've finished reading this book, you'll see why John Couch didn't just work for visionaries, he was one.

Steve Wozniak
Co-founder, Apple Computer

INTRODUCTION

"Life is always mysterious and surprising,
and you never know what's around the next corner."

—STEVE JOBS

Like Winston Churchill, Steve Jobs had a remarkable ability to inspire all who listened to him. On June 12, 2005, standing in front of a crowd of eager Stanford graduates, alumni, faculty, and friends, he delivered what many consider to be the most powerful words of his life, his "Stay Hungry, Stay Foolish" commencement speech. Like everyone else, I found it profound. Around the five-minute mark, as he looked back over his life, he said, "You can't connect the dots looking forward, you can only connect them looking backwards."

It was this idea of connecting the dots in our lives that, at 72 years old, inspired me to also look back on my life and career and begin connecting my own dots. As an Apple vice president for over 20 years, I've traveled the world, sharing Steve's vision with students, parents, teachers, educational leaders and even presidents of entire countries. During my journeys I am often asked in various languages many of the same questions such as "What was it like in the early days at Apple?" and "How was it working with Steve Jobs?" By sharing this book with you, my goal is to answer these questions and others that people never knew to ask.

WHAT TO EXPECT

The first chapter explores my educational and professional experiences that would act to prepare me for success in Apple's dynamic and challenging environment. You'll hear about the first time I was introduced to a computer while attending the University of California, Riverside, and how I became one of UC Berkeley's first 50 students to earn a computer science degree. You'll then follow me to Hewlett-Packard, where I got my first job as a software engineer working under the company's iconic CEO, Bill Hewlett. You'll learn about the time a young, ambitious visionary named Steve Jobs unexpectedly popped up at my house to try and convince me to leave HP, take a huge cut in pay, and join his promising startup, Apple Computer. Little did I know at the time that his startup would become the fastest growing company in the world in its first five years.

In chapters two and three you'll join me during Apple's earliest days, after I became the company's 54th employee, and find out what Steve did on my very first day that was so shocking it made me question whether or not I'd made a mistake. I'll share with you Apple's earliest culture and values as well as internal emails and documents, and you'll see why I was surprised how quickly I would be promoted to VP of Software. You will also join me on the trip I took with Steve and others to Xerox PARC, the now infamous visit that inspired us to rethink Apple and build two revolutionary computers.

Chapter four gives you a look at the early design and development of the Lisa computer and the challenges we faced during development of the Apple III. You'll hear about what Apple was like prior to, during, and after the company's initial public offering and join me inside Apple during the notorious "Black Wednesday."

Chapters five and six delve into a huge overhaul of Apple's organizational structure that led to my appointment as General

Manager and Vice President over the Lisa division. You'll find out what it was that disappointed Steve so much and how that feeling led to the birth of Macintosh. You'll hear the truth about what was behind the infamous bet Steve and I made, and I'll introduce you to "Lisa Technology" and the challenges of designing revolutionary hardware and making it work seamlessly with revolutionary software. You'll hear firsthand my conversation with Steve just after he made his "deal of the century" with Microsoft's Bill Gates and learn why Bill personally asked me to visit him at Microsoft headquarters.

Chapter seven covers Lisa's release, reception, successes, and perceived failings. You'll read about the similarities and differences between Lisa and Macintosh, and the influence both computers had on the future of personal computing. I'll also take you with me inside a meeting Steve and I had with John Sculley just before he became Apple's new CEO, and how you'll see just how much things changed.

Next, in chapters eight and nine, we'll look at the years I spent away from Apple, the reason I resigned, and how I may have unintentionally broken an SEC law. Finally, you'll hear about my perspective during Apple's "Dark Ages" and how I also struggled through my own dark age during the same time period. You'll go with me as I depart Apple and see how I led the successful turnaround of a failing school, why I took over as CEO of an innovative bioinformatics company, and how both of these experiences prepared me for my second tour of duty at Apple.

In chapters ten through twelve you'll see why Steve asked me to return to Apple, this time as the company's first Vice President of Education. You'll hear about all of the things my team and I did to stimulate the multibillion-dollar growth of Apple's education business, from research programs like ACOT (Apple Classrooms of Tomorrow), ACOT^2 (Apple Classrooms of Tomorrow, Today) and ConnectED, to marketing programs like

Kids Can't Wait, X for Teachers, Apple Distinguished Educators, programs like iTunes U and Apple Camp, and a Brazilian application development program that has since expanded around the world.

In chapters thirteen through fifteen you'll hear about the complexities of the Steve I knew from his earliest days right up until the sad day the world lost a visionary. You'll read stories never before told publicly, hear why Steve toasted our "20 years of friendship," and get my perspectives on his unrivaled focus, vision, and philanthropy. You'll meet Apple's other co-founder, my close friend, Steve "Woz" Wozniak, and what the biggest differences were between Woz and Jobs.

In the final chapter I'll take you inside Apple after Steve and share my perspective on the dramatic changes that took place. I'll walk you through the unfortunate dismantling of Apple's education division, an odd game of corporate musical chairs, and the controversy around the publication of my previous book, *Rewiring Education*, which ultimately led to my departure. Finally, the epilogue will bring you up to speed on my work after Apple. I'll also explain why education is an "infinite game," why it took a global pandemic to awaken education leaders to the importance of technology and teaching content within context, and the ways in which I have continued my fight to bring Steve's vision for education to life.

I am certainly fortunate to have been able to work with Steve Jobs at one of the most iconic companies in the world. As I connect the dots between my journey you will get a clear picture of how Apple made history. While some characterizations of Steve are more accurate than others, none have been able to adequately capture his complex human side as thoroughly as those of us who worked with him throughout Apple's rise, fall, and reincarnation. Hopefully this book will inspire you to "think different" and see that anything is possible.

CHAPTER 1

MENTAL BICYCLE

*"What a computer is to me is the most
remarkable tool that we've ever come up with.
It's the equivalent of a bicycle for our minds."*

—STEVE JOBS

Meeting Steve was no chance encounter. While I didn't know it at the time, the moment I started college would become the first dot that connected my life to the circumstances and events that led me to Apple, where I would manage the design and building of the first personal computer design with a graphical user interface (GUI). While this is not a biography of Steve, it's important that I share the stories of how our paths crossed not once, but twice.

My whirlwind journey started in 1968. At the time I was an undergraduate majoring in physics at the University of California, Riverside. In one of my junior year physics classes our professor gave us a final exam that consisted of just a single problem: "Describe the motion of a spinning top in free space." It was a daunting challenge because this problem had not been addressed in any lecture, nor was it covered in our textbook. Suddenly everyone in the class began to panic, including myself, because none of us had any clue on how to describe such a situation. It was not a solution that could be memorized, and I had not developed the skills to visualize this problem in ways that would allow me to derive the formula.

Prior to this, memorizing formulas had always been a successful strategy for me from high school right through my first few years of college. But this single problem had now made it clear that I would not be able to memorize my way through life, whether it be in college or in the workplace. I realized now that true learning wasn't about regurgitating facts and numbers but would come from my ability to critically evaluate and visualize complex problems. It was a humbling lesson that I would later rely on at Apple when Steve tasked me with building a personal computer that everyone could use and later to completely rewire education.

LINING UP THE DOTS

Later that same year at UC Riverside, I had my first experience with a computer in a class named Horticulture Science 120. Oddly enough, the horticulture department was one of the few departments that could afford an IBM computer and they were now offering an entry-level course on computer programming. My best friend, David Scott Easton, and I were curious to see what this new computer course was all about so we both decided to enroll. It didn't take long before I became captivated by the challenges of computer programming and the idea that there was never one correct answer. There was also no way to memorize answers because programming relied almost entirely on critical thinking and problem solving. I found it to be both challenging and exciting. This was the beginning of my infatuation with computers and programming which would later be referred to as *coding*. It was during this course that I decided that no matter what profession I ultimately chose, computer technology would have to play a significant role.

As I continued my studies at UC Riverside, not far away in the bordering city of Cupertino, California, an ambitious thirteen-year-old named Steve Jobs was looking for spare parts to build a "frequency counter." There was no internet in 1968 which meant his options in finding these parts were limited. Not one to be deterred, Steve naively decided that he would simply ask the CEO of a major technology company in the area for the spare parts he needed, not realizing that this was something that no one would ever do, and it was not supposed to be that easy. But apparently no one told Steve that. He already believed that anything was possible.

To that end, Steve called the largest technology company he could think of, Hewlett-Packard (HP), and boldly asked to speak with their co-founder and CEO, Bill Hewlett (who would soon become my own boss at HP). Somehow, he managed to get Bill on the phone and proceeded to ask for those spare parts. Bill was so impressed with this young kid's boldness and ambition that he agreed to give Steve the parts and also offered him a summer internship. This meant that as Steve entered his freshman year at Homestead High School, he would already be set up for a coveted HP internship at which he would be working on an HP assembly line building frequency counters. Bill Hewlett would later become a role model to Steve and an inspiration to him for years to come.

Back at UC Riverside, I was continuing to take the classes I needed to complete the requirements of my physics major. But I never felt an intrinsic love for it like I felt programming a computer. I really wanted to focus entirely on this emerging computer field. I wanted to switch majors but unfortunately UC Riverside didn't offer an undergraduate degree in computer science, which meant I would need to look elsewhere. Luckily, I didn't have to look far because coincidentally that same year an entire computer science department had opened just four-hundred miles away at UC Berkeley's College of Arts and Sciences. I now had a difficult decision to make. Should I continue with my undergraduate studies at UC Riverside, in which I had already invested three years? Or should I start over and follow my newfound passion for computer science, even though there was no guarantee that a brand-new academic program would even be able to keep up with this emerging and unpredictable industry?

I couldn't help at the time to remember the old African proverb, "Never test the depth of the water with both feet." But by the end of my junior year, I decided to ignore this wisdom. I married my college sweetheart and we both transferred to UC Berkeley, where I would begin building the foundation for a career in the computer industry.

UC BERKELEY

I left UC Riverside in 1969 after being accepted into UC Berkeley's Letters and Sciences' Department of Computer Science, where I earned an A.B. degree in just four quarters. I was then accepted into the Electrical Engineering and Computer Science Master's Program at Berkeley's College of Engineering and transferred back to the CS department as one of only *six* students accepted into the PhD program, and continued my studies there for an additional two and a half years.

After passing the preliminary exams and course work in the PhD program, the only requirement I had left was to complete a dissertation. Unfortunately, the department's faculty insisted I focus on "proving programs correct," which was of no interest to me. Over those last few years, as I worked toward my PhD, I found that I just wasn't as interested in theoretical research as much as I was in real world applications. I had become particularly fond of learning about computer user interfaces and error recovery, the tools that would allow non-technical individuals to be able to effectively use computers.

On May 15, 1969, I was dutifully working on a program-ming assignment on a Control Data 7600 computer system at Berkeley's Lawrence Hall of Science. While I was aware of the People's Park protests taking place on campus, I had no idea that that date would be forever remembered as "Bloody Thurs-day," the most violent confrontation in the university's histo-ry. What had started as peaceful rallies had suddenly turned into mass rioting with over 6,000 angry protesters wreaking havoc as they faced off against hundreds of police officers and more than 2,700 National Guard troops. I had stayed out of the protests because, while I was sympathetic to the anti-war movement, I believed societal change was more likely to come from technology than from street demonstrations. Consider-ing what took place that Thursday, it had been a good decision. My strong belief in the power of technology had convinced me that my career would be driven by the potential of the comput-er and software and I was anxious to get started.

After much consideration, I made the difficult decision to abandon my PhD studies and graduate with just an ABD (All But Dissertation) degree and I have no regrets. It was especially satisfying that I had now become one of Berkeley's first fifty graduates with a computer science degree, a distinction (and a key dot in my life) that would soon lead to meeting Steve Jobs and working for Apple Computer. Even today I find that this story seems to inspire others who feel as though they're on the wrong path whether academically or professionally. It amazes me just how many people choose to avoid following the well-worn footsteps of tradition. Years later, my Berkeley to Apple story would be highlighted in Todd Rose's best-sell-ing book, *Dark Horse*, which highlighted stories of people who went against the grain and successfully changed career paths at various points in their lives. At the end of my section in the book Rose wrote, "John decided to pursue personal fulfillment by harnessing his individuality, and thereby achieved profes-sional excellence."

STEVE WOZNIAK

In the midst of my graduating from UC Berkeley, fifty miles to the south a soon-to-be engineering prodigy, Steve Wozniak, was graduating from Homestead High School, the school that Steve Jobs was just starting to attend. The following year Woz would head off to Colorado to attend college but got expelled in his first year for hacking the school's computer system in order to more effectively conduct his notorious pranks. By 1971, after already having successfully built a personal computer, Woz also began attending UC Berkeley. He met Steve Jobs through a friend and, even though they were several years apart in age, the two found they had a lot in common, especially their love of technology.

Woz, the practical joker that he was, had already been using "borrowed" technology from phone manuals to create digital "blue boxes" that allowed him to make free, unlimited prank calls to anywhere in the world. Jobs was not a prankster like Woz but he did see potential in the blue boxes and convinced Woz that they should sell them. The fact that doing this was illegal didn't cross their minds. Decades later, Steve Jobs would say in interviews that if it had not been for Woz's blue boxes there would have been no Apple Computer.

BILL HEWLETT

In 1972, as Steve was leaving the Bay Area to attend Reed College in Oregon, I began working full time for Bill Hewlett at Hewlett-Packard where I programmed a large $250,000 computer. Bill was the CEO that Steve had gotten the spare parts from and offered him the internship just a few years earlier. But it was Dr. Tom Whitney, an engineering manager who oversaw the Advanced Development Labs became the HP 3000 lab manager whom I reported to. Tom's team at the Lab had developed the first handheld calculator, the HP-35, which was introduced in February 1972 for $395. The calculator was an extraordinary creation as it could add, subtract, divide and multiply in reverse Polish notation and also perform logarithmic and trigonometric functions.

Market research at the time had indicated that no one wanted, or would ever buy, a $395 calculator. But Bill Hewlett wanted one and insisted that it be built small enough to fit into his shirt pocket, something calculators at the time could not normally do. When the HP-35 was released, it was so successful that it completely disrupted the traditional slide rule market, showing the world that businesses should not rely solely on market research. One of my favorite quotes came from Ralph Waldo Emerson who said, "People can only see what they are prepared to see." In other words, market research is only valid when evaluating *existing* markets, but is irrelevant for those creating entirely new ones. It was a philosophy similar to one previously held by Henry Ford, founder of Ford Motor Company, who said that if he had relied on research and asked people what they really wanted, they would have said a faster horse. Not to rely on market research was one of several key philosophies Bill Hewlett operated by as he built HP and it would go on to influence many of my decisions at Apple.

A second memorable philosophy I learned from Bill during the five years I worked for him was, "More companies die/fail from indigestion than starvation." In other words, companies need to be careful to regulate the number of projects they take on. I would later share this lesson with Steve, who ended up creating his own variation of it when describing one of Apple's philosophies, "We take as much pride in the eight things that we don't do," he would say, "as the two that we do."

APPLE COMPUTER

By 1974 Steve had gotten his first job as an engineer at gaming company Atari, working for entrepreneur, Nolan Bushnell. While there, Steve paid Woz, who was still working at HP, to help him minimize the hardware required to create a prototype of a single-player version of Pong, a highly popular console game later renamed *Breakout*. Woz agreed to help, a key reason for the game's success. Jobs left Atari soon thereafter and began traveling throughout India in an effort to seek enlightenment, and later returned to an apple farm commune in Oregon.

On April 1, 1976, Steve Jobs, Steve Wozniak, and a third partner, Ronald Wayne, founded Apple Computer. The budding startup set up shop in Steve's garage where they sold a computer called Apple (later referred to as the Apple I) that was designed and hand-built by Woz. The Apple I came in the form of computer kits, introduced at the Personal Computing Festival in Atlantic City, New Jersey. They were being sold to computer hobbyists for exactly $666.66, due to Woz's fascination with repeating digits. The following year Apple was incorporated and showcased a prototype of their new Apple II computer at the West Coast Computer Faire, where it was a huge success.

I had heard about the Apple II while I was still working at HP. The idea of it was intriguing, but it was hard for me to imagine that a personal computer could exist at that point in time because of the shortcomings that would have needed to be addressed. The main one was that small business owners, as well as the majority of the general public, would have a difficult time finding people who could actually write programs for these computers. There wasn't a ton of programmers around at the time with this expertise. What was needed was what I referred to as a "datagramming" environment in which someone could define their data and the relationships required to solve problems, without having to learn to program a procedure-oriented language. One solution to this problem, which would not come about until 1978, was the "VisiCalc" application and others like "HyperCard" and visual programming arrived even later. As fascinated as I was with the idea behind a personal computer, a robust software environment would be required for Apple's new computer to be truly *personal*. As it turned out, someone else knew this as well.

MEETING STEVE

I was now working as a software section manager at Hewlett-Packard when I got a phone call from my former boss, Tom Whitney, saying he wanted me to meet Steve Jobs. After his work on the HP-35, Tom became the engineering manager in charge of the HP 3000 division, and I was now leading its software group. But in early 1978, Tom left HP to join Steve as Apple Computer's Vice President of Engineering. Apple only had around fifty employees at the time, including two high school software programmers who would come to work after school. It was clear to Tom that he needed more help on the software side and knew my background could be crucial to the company's success. On our call, Tom explained how the Apple II DOS operating system and Basic interpreter had been written by Woz. The only other software programs were utilities, a "Data Mover" that transferred data from a cassette recorder to memory, and one other minor application. He told me they needed help and wanted to arrange a lunch at his home where I could meet Steve. I wasn't seriously considering leaving HP but, because of my respect for Tom, I agreed to take the meeting.

The following week I drove up to Tom's house and was introduced to Steve. He was not what I was expecting. He was just

21 years old and looked younger. In contrast to my traditional slacks and white shirt, he wore a T- shirt, a pair of old Levi jeans and sockless Birkenstock sandals. He was a young man with intense eyes, long dark hair like hippies wore at the time and a complex enigma. He looked more like a Hollywood actor than a computer entrepreneur and certainly nothing like anyone I was used to seeing at HP. I liked the way he thought big.

Right from the start Steve began passionately sharing his vision with deep intensity and enthusiasm that I found to be infectious. He was more persuasive and inspiring than any-one I had ever met before. His every word had so much fervor that they drew me more and more into his ambitious vision for Apple. This was akin to a single-minded obsession to make computers available to everyone in the world. By doing so, he wanted, expected even, to make Apple the most significant technology company in history. There was zero doubt in his mind that this would happen, it was only a matter of how long it was going to take.

I found Steve to be so utterly inspiring that in a single conversation, devoid of details, he had me sitting on the edge of my seat with excitement. Steve, eight years younger than me, began talking about changing the world and I was con-vinced he would. There was now no doubt in *my* mind that this was going to happen, not because of some brilliant plan, but because he was going to *will* it to happen one way or another. What I found most intriguing though was his innate ability to communicate his vision through stories, analogies, and meta-phors.

As I sat across from him on the couch, Steve explained his vision for the personal computer by relaying his interpre-tation of an article he read in the magazine *Scientific American*. It was based on a study that measured the efficiency of loco-motion for various species on the planet. The study noted that the condor used the least energy to move a kilometer, while humans were somewhat unimpressive, coming in a third of the way down the list. But the article's writer had the foresight to test the efficiency of locomotion for a human riding a bicycle. Suddenly, the human on the bicycle surpassed the condor and topped the charts. "That's what a computer is," Steve said. "It's the most remarkable tool mankind has ever come up with, equivalent to a bicycle for our minds. In the same way a bicycle amplifies our physical ability, technology can amplify our intellectual potential. The concept of a personal computer as a *mental* bicycle really captured my attention and has stuck with me ever since."

DECISIONS, DECISIONS

By the end of my initial conversation with Steve I was sold. I knew this scrappy young entrepreneur was going to do something special and possibly revolutionize the computer industry. My decision to leave Hewlett-Packard to help make this vision a reality was not an easy one. HP was one of the biggest, most influential technology companies in the world. Getting a job there was highly competitive and seen as one of the holy grails for technology jobseekers. Apple, on the other hand, was barely known and, as a startup, would be a risky endeavor to undertake. I was also making $65,000 plus bonuses at HP and was a candidate for Tom Whitney's old engineering manager position, which would have come with significantly more pay and benefits. In contrast, the maximum salary at Apple at the time, from the CEO down, was $40,000. Steve told me he wanted to hire only individuals who shared his vision rather than someone who viewed Apple as an economic opportunity.

He promised me Apple stock but also fully expected me to take that $25,000 pay cut. I would also be going from managing a large team of software engineers to managing no one. My decision was even tougher because I had a family to consider and making such a big change would come with significant risk. Our conversation ended with my promising to consider the offer and get back to him. But much to my surprise, a few days later he dropped by my house unannounced in an effort to follow up on his offer. He had brought an Apple II computer with him, which he sat proudly on my kitchen table. He then looked over at my four-year-old son, Kris, and said, "You can keep this if your dad comes to work for me." It was a shrewd move!

Kris became consumed with that Apple II and never wanted to turn it off. Our television didn't turn on at all that weekend, as he was too busy playing with this cool new, *interactive* tool. My son was riding that mental bicycle to places I didn't know a four-year-old could go! Nonetheless, I had to warn him not to get *too* attached to it, because if I decided to turn the job down, I would have to return the computer. Kris looked absolutely horrified by the mere thought of such a thing. Finally, that Sunday night just before bed, he looked up at me with those four-year-old pleading eyes of his and said, "Just say yes, Daddy."

CURVE 68

Another big factor that played a role in my decision on whether to join Steve or remain at HP, was HP's reliance on a specific method of compensation. It was called Curve 68 and it based each employee's pay on "years since first degree." This policy ended up limiting the salary options for recent graduates, many of whom could already program circles around seasoned HP programmers. It was discouraging because potential hires could look a few years into the future and realize that their growth at HP would be based on longevity rather than ability, which was never an appealing option for highly talented people.

Aside from working at HP at the time, I was also teaching two courses at San Jose State, "Compiler Construction Theory and Practice," and "Language Directed Machine Design." While there, I witnessed firsthand an example of Curve 68's restrictions. One of my students, Richard Page, had a job at Fairchild Semiconductor as a micro-coder working with the F8 processor. In my class I had used a theoretical machine, Algol Object Code, that was designed by Professor Jim Morris at UC Berkeley. The assignment in my compiler course was for students to write an interpreter for the AOC code and a compiler that then generated the code for the AOC theoretical machine. But Richard went beyond what the assignment required and actually wrote software that completely interpreted the theoretical code to run on an F8 processor. It was quite impressive. I had always wanted to hire people at HP who were smarter than myself and it was clear to me that Richard fit the bill.

Meanwhile, Ed McCracken, the manager of the HP 3000 division had just defined ten major objectives for our team. One of these was to put the Scan and Move instructions for a Cobol compiler into microcode, which would speed up execution. It was not an easy task to accomplish and promised to also be quite time-consuming. Management searched for nine months for someone they could hire who could do the job, but found no one, at least until I brought Richard in for an interview.

HP's engineering managers had estimated that at best it would take someone at least fourteen months to code the project, but Richard, who was already highly regarded and well paid at Fairchild, assured us that he could do it in just six months. I was highly impressed and ended up offering him $100 over the Curve 68 rate. But much to my dismay, our HR department rejected my offer as being "above the guidelines."

I went to our head of HR, Ken Coleman and said, "This project is one of Ed's top 10 priorities and the position has been open for over nine months!" He just looked at me as I continued, "Now I've finally found someone who can do the whole project in *six* months instead of fourteen and you're going to deny my offer for a measly $100 a month above guidelines?" Ken just shrugged, still saying nothing. "Well then I'll just have to go ask Ed to override your decision," I said, which finally got his attention. "You wouldn't really do that, would you?" he asked. "In a split second!" I snapped. Although Ken did ultimately agree, it was a battle that should have never happened, and I knew it wouldn't have happened with Steve at Apple. Richard was hired at HP, but ended up following me to Apple, becoming the company's first technical fellow, and years later would join Steve at NeXt.

While the Curve 68 debacle was frustrating, in the end it was Steve's passion and his vision of personal computers as mental bicycles that made the difference in my decision. "Everything I have is from someone else's contribution, the house I live in, the car I drive, the clothes I wear and the food I eat," he told me at the time. "I want to give something back." Like I had come to believe, Steve knew that technology would be the one thing that would empower people and change their lives forever. We both agreed that personal computers should not be something that took us places we've already been, but instead they would allow us to explore, innovate, and create the future. "When you run a company, you have to get people to buy into your dreams," Steve told me. "Which is why I try and get people to see what I see." He certainly did a good job of that with me, because I completely bought into his ambitious vision and I knew that with my programming skills I could help him bring it to life. A week after our meeting I became Apple's 54th employee.

CHAPTER 2

EMPLOYEE #54

*"We hire people who want to make
the best things in the world."*

—STEVE JOBS

Not long after agreeing to join Apple, Steve invited me to Cupertino to meet the execs, who included CEO Mike Scott aka "Scotty," co-founder Steve Wozniak, head of sales Gene Carter, head of marketing Phil Roybal, and the company's initial investor, Mike "ACM" Markkula. I was really impressed with Mike, who was an engineering major out of USC and a seasoned marketing manager from Intel where stock options made him a millionaire by the age of 33. As a computer science major, I found a kindred spirit in Mike, who also loved to dabble with Basic coding. In fact, he started to code some of the original application software for the Apple II, which included a financial planner and a tax planner.

Mike would become an ardent supporter of mine as he had for many of Apple's early employees. At one point he shared with me his thinking on company organization. He explained how startup tech companies are always engineering focused, but when they come to the realization that their products aren't generating enough revenue, they reorganize and instead begin focusing on marketing and sales. Then they realize that they're no longer creating innovative new products and they flip back to engineering again. Mike's goal at Apple, he said, was to always focus on both at the same time.

In my last interview, Scotty, Apple's CEO, asked me what I thought were the two biggest challenges the company was facing. The first was software, I said, because Apple lacked the expertise to develop software that would be needed to actually sell systems. Ironically, six months later I was promoted to VP of Software. Second, I told him that I thought manufacturing was another big challenge because it wasn't clear whether Apple had the capability required to keep up with what I knew was going to be immense demand. He agreed with both and seemed excited that I was joining the team.

I was initially hired as Apple's first Director of New Products and reported directly to Steve, who had given himself the role of VP of New Products. Together we made up Apple's product marketing team, responsible for defining all new and future products. I actually began work in October 1978 but didn't receive an official written offer right away, mostly because doing paperwork was not one of Steve's strengths. By the time I finally got my written offer, on November 6th, I had already been hard at work for weeks.

Apple Computer, Inc.
10260 Bandley Drive
Cupertino, California 96014

6 November 1978

Dear John,

This is to confirm in writing our offer of employment at Apple Computer in the position of New Product Manager. This position reports directly to the Vice President of New Product Development and has the responsibility for defining, managing and tracking all new products within specific product lines. Your responsibility will include managing the entire LISA product line. In compensation for the above responsibility, Apple offers you:

1. *A salary of $40,000/year.*

2. *A guaranteed $5,000/year raise, effective in 6 months.*

3. *A stock option of Ten Thousand (10,000) shares of Apple stock at $3.00/share under the Apple Stock Option Plan, with 2,500 shares available for immediate purchase, subject to Apple Board of Directors approval.*

4. *Apple will make the funds available for such purchase via a full recourse note.*

Congratulations for joining the fastest growing computer company in the world.

Steven Jobs
Vice President, New Product Development

CULTURE SHOCK

My initial task at Apple was to evaluate and procure peripherals for the Apple II. I worked with Steve to find and meet third-party vendors that could add value to the Apple II product line. My first two meetings were with a printer manufacturer and a modem company and were conducted in the original Apple building, Bandley One. During the first, a couple of printer representatives showed up in well-pressed suits and ties. I escorted them into a small conference room where we all sat and waited for Steve, who showed up late. We all watched in shock as Steve finally came strolling in, barefoot, wearing a wrinkled T-shirt along with a pair of old blue jeans with holes in both knees.

He then climbed up and sat in lotus position directly in the middle of the conference table. I didn't know what to make of what I was seeing, as something like this would have been unimaginable at HP. Steve then took the small thermal printer from the representatives, studied it a moment and then glanced at both of the gentlemen. "This is a piece of shit," he told them. He then climbed off of the table and casually walked out of the room. The total meeting time was less than five minutes. I looked over at our two guests, shrugged and said, "Well uh, thanks for coming." As I showed them out, I apologized and began wondering whether I had made the right decision in joining Apple. *What have I gotten myself into?* I thought.

We then had another meeting scheduled that same day with a different vendor. This time I had to mentally prepare myself because I had no idea what Steve was going to say or do. This meeting was with Dennis Hayes, one of the founders of DC Hayes Modem. He and his partner, Dale Heatherington, were well-known and respected in the tech industry for having invented the PC modem a year earlier. Dennis was the more business-minded of the two which is why he was the one making the visit. When he arrived, I ushered him in to the conference room and we waited. Steve came in and once again climbed onto the middle of the conference table and sat in lotus position. I remember thinking, *Uh oh, here we go again.* He picked up the shiny black "Micro Modem II," studied it for all of 15 seconds and said, "I'll take a million."

Dennis, practically choking, looked at me incredulously and explained that they were a young company, incorporated a few months earlier, and were not capable yet of producing a million modems. I told him not to worry and that we'd figure something out. After this second meeting, it was understood that in Steve's world things were always either *this* or *that*. Good or bad. Insanely great or a piece of shit. There were no grey areas, and he knew right away what he wanted. Apple did end up using the DC Hayes modem and did so with great success.

For years after that meeting, I watched as Steve maintained that same dress code for himself. It wouldn't be until Apple's IPO that he began dressing in Wilkes Bashford clothing, and then eventually to his famous black turtleneck. For me it was a relief that I could wear a pair of Levi's, a shirt without a tie, and Birkenstocks to work. It was Steve and Apple, back in the early 70s, that set the casual dress code for what Silicon Valley entrepreneurs and programmers continue to wear today, although most do tend to usually wear shoes. We knew early on that wearing a suit didn't make any of us smarter or move the company any closer to success.

After my first week at Apple, I could already tell it was going to be challenging working with Steve and adjusting to such a breakneck, innovative pace. But I loved it for those very reasons and couldn't wait to see how much of a difference we would be able to make in the world. As we headed full steam toward 1979, every day we were making tremendous progress and as we moved closer to reaching our goals, I began to comprehend that this was indeed the opportunity of a lifetime. I had spent years preparing for this job without even realizing it and from my very first day I knew that I was now a part of something extraordinary.

TRIP HAWKINS

At some point in 1978, a fellow named Trip Hawkins was hired by Mike Markkula as Apple's Director of Strategy and Marketing and was given the task of updating Apple's marketing plan. Trip was a key part of the initial Apple team and came with impressive credentials. As an undergraduate at Harvard University, he designed his own major called "Strategy and Applied Game Theory," then attended Stanford Business School, and finally joined Apple as its 68th employee.

Trip would also become the original director of marketing for Lisa but would end up leaving the company before its introduction to launch a startup video game publisher called Electronic Arts (EA), which today is worth over $40 billion. But in early 1979, while Trip was still at Apple, he had completed and distributed a draft of a new marketing plan to key employees. I felt he did an excellent job capturing the competitive landscape at the time and defining Apple's initial marketing objectives. The plan read:

> 1979 promises to be the most difficult year of Apple's history. At least four corporations will enter the personal computing market. TI, Atari and Mattel have all made firm decisions to participate. Several Japanese firms, notably Sanyo, Matsushita and Toshiba, have shown impressive prototype units. Commodore, Bally, Cromemco and Ohio Scientific will have a noticeable presence in various market segments and cannot be counted completely out. Radio Shack, having emerged in 1978 as the market leader, will attempt to maintain its position with the TRS-80 while developing additional products and a new chain of Computer Stores.

Apple's Situation

Key Strengths heading into 1979 are:

- Image as "Cadillac" personal computer firm, including the product, support and marketing efforts
- More than two years of experience distributing computers through retail channels
- The ability to deliver more floppy disk drives than any other company in the industry

Apple's relative weaknesses are:

- Inability of existing Apple II to allow penetration of truly consumer distribution channels
- Inadequate application software
- Inability to meet schedules

Apple's Objectives for 1979:

1. Maintain image as #1 in assembled hoppy computer market
2. Become a leading supplier to educational institutions
3. Establish the Apple name in the business market and prepare the potential customer base for Lisa. (early 1980)
4. Maintain visibility and participation among consumers through media emphasizing through "Cadillac" image until Apple can offer a true consumer product. (mid 1980)

5. Become a dominant supplier of floppy-disk based personal computers.
6. Establish a strong OEM customer base.
7. Rapidly procure and develop applications software, focusing on business and educational markets.
8. Become the leader and expert at selling computers through independent retail distribution channels.

GROWTH SPURT

Whenever I'm asked what Apple was like in the early days my typical response is that it was fast and furious. The rate of growth during that time was astronomical. Within the first five years Apple had reached $100 million in sales, becoming America's fastest growing company. With that growth rate it took everything we had to try and keep up. Sometimes we struggled to procure enough building space to handle the growth and even when we did, we'd be lucky to get building approvals quick enough. New employees were being hired so fast that they were practically sitting on each other! At one point Steve got so frustrated while waiting for a building approval that he rented mobile trailers and turned them into makeshift offices complete with California license plates.

A second example of the rapid growth we experienced happened after we decided to set up a new manufacturing facility in Carlton, Texas. Immediately after making the decision, we began placing ads looking for manufacturing employees, by the second week we were conducting interviews, and by the fourth week our new hires were already manufacturing and producing Apple II computers. It was an incredibly fast turnaround by anyone's standards.

Yet another growth-related challenge for us was that it was difficult to get telephones installed in a timely manner, an issue that set us back even more than our lack of office space. At one point I was giving a presentation to a dozen AT&T executives at a retreat in Colorado. Since I had the "phone guys" right in front me, I decided to call them out for not being able to keep up with Apple's demand in Silicon Valley: "How is it we can build a manufacturing plant and have Apple IIs coming off of a manufacturing line faster than you guys can install a phone?" Even though I said it jokingly, they knew it was true. Shortly after that meeting, several of those executives sent me their resumes, hoping to jump off the AT&T ship and join Apple.

APPLE'S VALUES AND CULTURE

While the pace during Apple's growth spurt was stressful, it was also exciting and made for a very interesting culture. Every year we were hiring more people than the previous year, but the rapid speed, long hours, and high expectations definitely weren't for everyone. It made for a relatively high turnover rate, mostly because, in our rush to hire, we were bringing in some people with misaligned values and expectations of a corporate culture that weren't representative of Apple. What we were doing was so unique that it was actually challenging for us to define a single set of values and to explain exactly our culture. We would eventually document our values and expectations, and to ensure that all new employees knew and understood them, we completely revised and updated our new manager onboarding program. Our first "Apple Values" documentation consisted of nine key areas:

1. **Empathy for Customers/Users**: We offer superior products that fill real need and provide

lasting value. We deal fairly with competitors and meet customers and vendors more than halfway. We are genuinely interested in solving customer problems and will not compromise our ethics or integrity in the name of profit.

2. **Achievement/Aggressiveness**: We set aggressive goals and drive ourselves hard to achieve them. We recognize that this is a unique time, when our products will change the way people work and live. It's an adventure and we're on it together.

3. **Positive Social Contribution**: As a corporate citizen, we wish to be an economic, intellectual, and social asset in communities where we operate. But beyond that, we expect to make this world a better place to live. We build products that extend human capability, freeing people from drudgery and helping them achieve more than they could alone.

4. **Innovation/Vision**: We built our company on innovation, providing products that were new and needed. We accept the risks inherent in following our vision, and work to develop leadership products which command the profit margins we strive for.

5. **Individual Performance**: We expect individual commitment and performance above the standard for our industry. Only then will we make the profits that permit us to seek our other corporate objectives. Each employee can and must make a difference for in the final analysis,

INDIVIDUALS determine the character and strength of Apple.

6. **Team Spirit**: Teamwork is essential to Apple's success, for the job is too big to be done by any one person. Individuals are encouraged to interact with all levels of management, sharing ideas and suggestions to improve Apple's effectiveness and quality of life. It takes all of us to win. We support each other and share the victories and rewards together. We're enthusiastic about what we do.

7. **Quality/Excellence**: We care about what we do. We build into Apple products a level of quality, performance, and value that will earn the respect and loyalty of customers.

8. **Individual Reward**: We recognize each person's contribution to Apple's success, and we share the financial rewards that flow from high performance. We recognize also that rewards must be psychological as well as financial and strive for an atmosphere where each individual can share the adventure and excitement of working at Apple.

9. **Good Management**: The attitudes of managers toward their people are of primary importance. Employees should be able to trust the motives and integrity of their supervisors. It is the responsibility of management to create a productive environment where Apple values flourish.

Later, Apple Values were simplified in what we referred to as the Apple Quality of Life Project. Our revised values were listed as:

- One person, one computer.
- We are going for it and we will set aggressive goals.
- We are all on the adventure together.
- We build products we believe in.
- We are here to make a positive difference in society, as well as make a profit.
- Each person is important; each has the opportunity and the obligation to make a difference.
- We are all in it together, win or lose.
- We are enthusiastic!
- We are creative; we set the pace.
- We want everyone to enjoy the adventure we are on together.
- We care about what we do.
- We want to create an environment in which Apple values flourish.

BANNERS OF INNOVATION

The first person to run Apple's human resources department failed horribly, because he completely misunderstood our culture. At one point he sent a memo around saying he had implemented a new rule stating that from this point forward Apple would only reimburse the moving expenses for recruits that lived over fifty miles away. That meant that even though Apple was in the heart of Silicon Valley, with Stanford less than fifty miles away, and UC Berkeley fifty-seven miles away, I would be able to offer moving expenses to UC Berkeley graduates, but not to Stanford graduates. It made no sense and was a ridiculous change. "You don't get it," I told him. "We don't follow inflexible rules and regulations around here, we operate through relationships." He completely disagreed and "left" Apple within weeks.

Our next head of human resources was Ann Bowers, a very bright woman who actually did understand Apple's culture and what we were trying to accomplish. Ann was the wife of Ed Noyce, co-founder of Intel Corp, the large semiconductor chip manufacturer whose headquarters was based in nearby Santa Clara, CA. I especially liked that she was open to new ways of doing things and that she always encouraged employee feedback. She and I had several meetings about the caliber of people we needed to hire and the processes that would be needed to orientate new managers. Prior to Ann's arrival, I had created what I referred to as my "Banners of Innovation," a set of principles and expressions meant to easily communicate Apple's creative culture and motivate my team. These banners included phrases like:

- If there is a light at the end of the tunnel, some else has already been there
- Let's not argue about diamonds or emeralds when the world has coal
- The Reward is in the Journey
- Know the difference between effort and results
- Inspire don't require
- A different viewpoint is worth 100 IQ points
- Believe in miracles but don't schedule them
- It's more fun to be a pirate than to join the Navy
- Throw creativity at the project, not the checkbook

I was glad to see that Ann loved the banners and we began using them as a way to jumpstart our new onboarding program that we were now calling Apple University, which now consisted of a full week of new employee training and was mostly intended for new managers. The goal was to inspire them to think differently rather than follow the well-worn footsteps of tradition. Far too often people would come to Apple with the attitudes and cultures of their previous experiences and employers. In their minds, if they came from a company with an organization based on a division structure, then Apple should also be organized around divisions. If they came from an HR department with numerous polices and regulations, then that's what they wanted to put in place at Apple. This type of rigid mindset was the reason we rarely hired people from IBM, whose culture was just so opposite.

One of the things we wanted to do with Apple University was get the point across to new hires that we were creating a new market, so they needed to leave their preconceived ideas at the door. We did several things to ensure this was clear, but one of the most memorable was a game Ann and I played that kicked things off. On the first day of the new managers' class, Ann would arrive slightly late wearing a three-piece suit and tie, carrying a briefcase and a stack of business management books. I would then say to her, "Welcome to Apple, there's a seat up front and by the way, our dress code here is a bit less formal." She got to the desk and then "accidentally" dropped the books she was carrying.

As I began helping her pick them up, I told her she would not need the business plan from her previous company or any of the management books, because they were the antithesis of Apple's culture and that we were moving in directions never before explored. Every time we did that, I watched as many of the new recruits began quietly hiding the business plans and management books that *they* had brought too. After the routine I shared our Banners of Innovation with them and, by the end of their very first class, they understood that Apple was unique and in order for them to succeed there, they had to be able to think differently. The Banners of Innovation had made onboarding new hires a lot smoother and I was proud of the work that Ann and I did on them. I've always felt honored to have been the executive who got to open the original Apple University.

CHAPTER 3

THE EARLY DAYS

"One of the things that made Apple great was that,
in the early days, it was built from the heart."

—STEVE JOBS

In March 1979, five months into my employment, I was asked to take on the role of VP of Software, an area that had been neglected due to Apple's heavy focus on Apple II and Apple III hardware and peripherals. Prior to creating the Apple Disk in 1978, Woz had designed and developed a printer board, a serial communications board, a PAL APPLE II and an Arabic APPLE II. Along with his friend John Draper, he had earlier developed a phone board code named "Charlie board" in a private office away from Apple management. According to Woz, the functionality of the board was "unequalled for 12 years but never became an Apple product because others at Apple did not trust Draper."

In comparison, Apple's software offerings were limited. On Apple's software price list, Hank Smith, an investor and board member, had written a note to me in the margin, the not-so-subtle words, "This is pitiful, good luck, move fast." It was true, Apple needed software badly and quickly. Other outside board members, Art Rock, Henry Singleton, and Don Valentine echoed similar challenges and it was evident how the inside board members Steve, Mike and Scotty knew I had the software experience to help.

SOFTWARE PLANS

My initial focus in this new position was to create a software plan that would strategically unite Apple's hardware and software products. The plan for the Apple II's consumer market was "the more the better," which meant encouraging software developers with procedure-oriented languages (Pascal, Fortran, etc.) to develop new applications or port new applications for the Apple II and Apple III. For Apple III's small business market, which was in initial development, the plan was to develop a new operating system with a file system that would support Pascal and additional procedure-oriented languages. Then there was this idea for a computer we called "Lisa" that was going to be designed for the corporate market, but up to this point the computer only existed in our dreams. The plan for Lisa sounded simple but would be extremely challenging— to design a computer that *anyone* could use.

Just prior to my starting at Apple, Steve had told me about Lisa, which was a code name, he said, for a revolutionary computer he wanted to design. It was actually one of many code names we used publicly when referring to Apple projects. The Apple III was called "Sara," named after its designer Wendall Sander's daughter. There was also a small, relatively unknown, project called "Annie," and then there was "Lisa," named after Steve's daughter, who was born a few months prior to my arrival. For whatever reason, Steve didn't want the public to know that the computer was named after his daughter, so in an effort to keep it private, we concocted a phony acronym, telling the media that LISA stood for: "Locally Integrated Software Architecture." It meant absolutely nothing, but it sure sounded cool.

My first priority as VP of Software was to work on the Apple II. It was our only publicly available computer and generated all of Apple's revenue, but it also desperately needed more applications. So, first and foremost, I needed to figure out how to maximize the number of applications that could run on it, or as Steve more explicitly said, "I want *every* application in the world to run on the Apple II." The irony was that Steve didn't believe that standards and compatibility were important and felt that all they did was inhibit creativity and innovation.

But I was now tasked with doing just that by ensuring the Apple II could run every application and, even worse, he wanted it done by Christmas! "Steve, we don't have a monopoly on creativity," I told him, insisting that achieving such a lofty goal could not be done through in-house means alone. I told him that what I really needed was to be able to leverage the creativity of others by designing a third-party development program that would encourage outside developers to write applications for both the Apple II and Apple III. He would eventually agree that developing such a program was the way to go, so I hired a friend, Mike Kane, to join my team and tasked him with overseeing the program's creation.

BILL BUDGE

To ensure that the new program was a success I wanted to convince my friends at UC Berkeley and Hewlett-Packard to write software robust applications that could successfully take advantage of the growing market for personal computers. The first person I reached out to about this was Bill Budge, who had purchased an Apple II while still a student at UC Berkeley and had already written games for it, which included a cool Atari Pong clone called Penny Arcade. I reached out to him and was glad to hear he was still interested in becoming a professional video game programmer. I knew that this would be a great opportunity to boost our Apple II applications, because even then games were some of the best-selling software applications.

Today, when any new hardware systems are introduced, their developers will often turn to games first, in order to quickly go mainstream, and when that happens, they leverage the game's success as a way to introduce non-game applications.

Luckily, I was able to convince Bill to trade a number of his game programs for a Centronics printer, promising him I would put his programs on the DOS disk that shipped with every Apple II—an early form of bundling that other software companies like Microsoft would later implement. I told Bill this arrangement would introduce his work to millions of consumers and make him a "Software Hero." He liked that idea and agreed to the trade, which helped accelerate both his and Apple II's path to success. He would also go on to create tools and graphic libraries that helped other game designers add to Apple II's growing software library.

Shortly after Bill and I came to an agreement, he shared with me his latest game effort, Pinball. I played it and initially loved it, but it did become a bit redundant after playing it awhile. I told him that it was fun but that I feared people might get bored too quickly. I suggested he make it a bit more interactive, such as allowing players to be able to change the numbers of spinners, bumpers and balls. He liked the idea a lot, got straight to work on it, and was able to relatively quickly develop what he called the "Pinball Construction Kit." It was one of the first interactive computer games that gave players the opportunity to change things inside the game itself, allowing them to have new experiences each time they played. Today many popular games like Minecraft, Roblox, and Fortnite, have this kind of functionality, but back then it was an incredibly novel concept. Just as I had predicted, Bill would go on to be recognized as Apple's first, third-party *Software Hero*.

As Bill Budge continued creating compatible games, Apple was also developing other types of software applications that included: Apple Post, Apple Writer, Dow Jones Portfolio Manager, Shell Games, Apple PLOT and Cashier. The first accounting software, Controller, was developed by Dakin 5 in Colorado and, for Apple, it became a critical application. But the application that would come to play the most significant role in increasing Apple II sales, was called Visicalc, the world's first spreadsheet application. I was so impressed with the application's versatility that I gave a free Apple II to both of its creators, Dan Bricklin and Dan Flystra. I wanted to do everything possible to ensure that Apple hardware would be the first to implement Visicalc software. It was also becoming clear that Visicalc had the potential to be a type of "datagramming" model that would be needed in order to empower non-programmers to solve problems without having to learn a procedure-oriented language.

APPLICATION DEVELOPMENT

Another thing we did to encourage more application development for the Apple II was provide developers with additional programming environments other than just DOS and Basic. In the summer of 1979 Apple cut a licensing deal with UC San Diego (UCSD) that gave us the rights to market UCSD Pascal on Apple hardware in exchange for forty Apple IIs, to be used in their student lab. This too-good-to-be-true deal was made possible by the fact that Bill Atkinson, one of Apple's top programmers, had graduated from UCSD. It also helped that Jef Raskin, Apple's Director of Publications, who Steve had hired to write the Apple II's BASIC programming manual, also had key contacts at the school.

At one point, Jef and Brian Howard, who co-wrote the Pascal manual, had noticed that the syntax chart published in earlier manuals was incorrect. They worked together to create a new color-coded syntax poster to aid in the understanding of Pascal's language. The posters were actually a huge hit with developers, as I frequently found them hanging over their desks. Once the UCSD Pascal deal closed I traveled to Zurich to meet Professor Niklaus Wirth, the highly respected creator of Pascal. It was a great honor to meet him and I was thrilled that by the end of our meeting I had his permission to use his name in our marketing efforts. This gave Apple more credibility with third-party programmers and full access to the first high-level language, other than BASIC, for the personal computer.

I was even able to persuade Professor Wirth to autograph my own personal copy of a Pascal poster! Steve saw that the poster would be a great promotional vehicle for marketing *Apple Pascal,* so he had a professional artist redraw it in 3D. In typical Steve Jobs style, he had the artist change the colors on the poster, which made the chart lose its programming functionality. Steve did not inform Jef about this change, so Jef didn't learn about it until well after thousands were printed. It was too late for Jef to complain and, even if he did, there wasn't much he could have done about it. Steve assured him that the new design looked much better than the original despite its lack of programming functionality. This was a good example of how much Steve appreciated and prioritized design and appearance over functionality.

THE LISA PROJECT

When I first arrived at Apple, the company was working on just two computers, the Apple II and Apple III. The Apple III was designed to be an evolutionary computer for the small business market. It was supposed to be the successor to the Apple II and run the former computer's software while addressing its shortcomings. Since I was still just Director of New Products at the time, I had little to do with the Apple III, but I knew that it was plagued with hardware problems, which caused many of us to worry that it could potentially have major problems when shipped. I never put a whole lot of thought into the Apple III though, because Steve made it clear that he recruited me to work on revolutionary, not evolutionary computers.

The computer I was most interested in, and expected to be working on, was Lisa. Steve had told me that *that* was the one that needed to be revolutionary and he specifically wrote in my offer letter that one of my responsibilities would be "managing the entire LISA product line." I couldn't wait to get started but soon realized that not only was there no Lisa, there also wasn't a clear definition of what Lisa was even supposed to look like! The Lisa computer had actually been little more than an *idea* that Steve had long been envisioning. Luckily, by the time I was promoted to VP of Software, Lisa was at least opened as an official Apple project, meaning I could finally begin defining its software strategy and functionality. In order to do this effectively I knew I would need to work closely with our hardware team in order to ensure that the computer itself would be able to actually run revolutionary software.

In the spring of 1979, I sat down with Steve and Trip Hawkins to discuss our vision for Lisa. We decided it needed to be a powerful and intuitive enough machine that corporate "knowledge workers" (i.e., office workers and managers) could turn it on and figure out in a matter of minutes what to do, without needing a manual. As much as Steve loved the Apple II and fostered such high expectations for the Apple III, he still felt the learning curve for using them was too high for people with little technical experience. Computers back then were running on operating systems that utilized command-line instructions, which were intimidating and confusing to many would-be users. Even just turning on computers presented users with nothing other than a black screen and a flashing white vertical line waiting for typed instructions. Users who didn't know what to type were unable to use the computer. Even those who did know the proper instructions were still limited on what they could actually do.

Steve Wozniak, Apple's other co-founder, was already considered to be one of the best and most respected engineers in Silicon Valley. After designing the Apple I and Apple II, he was supposed to become the lead designer on Lisa, but since Apple did not yet have a plan for it, there was nothing for him to design and by the time I arrived he had already moved on to other projects. This meant that rather than working directly with Woz, which I had been really looking forward to, I ended up working with Ken Rothmuller, a former HP manager who I had previously worked with prior to our joining Apple.

Ken now worked in Tom Whitney's engineering department and I was told that he was the head of "Lisa hardware," which I figured must have been a pretty easy job considering there *was* no Lisa hardware. Even so, Ken had his own vision for what he thought Lisa hardware should look like, but it did not match Steve's or my own. Ken's vision for Lisa's hardware wasn't revolutionary at all and seemed more like a souped-up Apple III. He regularly made the case that Lisa should maintain keyboard shortcuts and function keys, the same functionality that was deployed on many of the HP calculators and terminals.

To be fair, neither Steve nor I knew at the time what revolutionary computer hardware and software should look like, but we had been very clear on what it *shouldn't* look like. I also knew that if it was going to empower non-programmers then it needed to break away from the textual command-line, support higher-level languages, and be able to run much more sophisticated software. A lot more memory was going to be needed as well as a much faster 16-bit processor capable of keeping up with resource-intensive software. But Ken didn't agree and continued to argue for his more traditional view of Lisa, even after Steve had made it clear multiple times that what he wanted was something completely revolutionary. Ken had always been a dependable colleague and friend, but no matter how hard I tried I could not persuade him to think differently when it came to Lisa's hardware design. Nonetheless, it was ultimately my responsibility to present to Steve what Lisa should look like and that's what I intended to do.

XEROX PARC

In December of 1968, a well-respected engineer and inventor named Douglas Engelbard was scheduled to give a public presentation that he referred to as "The Mother of all Demos." It was a grandiose name but certainly fitting for the things that Engelbard would be presenting. He was about to introduce to the world a few quirky things that he had designed while working at the SRI International Research Institute. As the crowd sat restless in anticipation, Engelbard unveiled technologies that would turn out to be the precursors for a graphical user interface (GUI) and a computer mouse. At the time of his demo no one had ever seen either of these things before, and they were both quite revolutionary.

As amazing of a spectacle that the presentation was, once it was over, some people began to question the usefulness of his inventions, primarily because the computer he was using to showcase them was so large and bulky that it seemed to many as though they would not be very practical. Nonetheless, there was a group of Xerox Corporation executives at the demo who immediately recognized the potential of Englebard's inventions. Xerox had been around since 1906, but only recently began making a conscious effort to expand their technology-based research and development division. They now believed that they had just witnessed the future and they had every intention of owning it. They wanted to create more practical versions of Englebard's inventions but doing so would have taken a lot of time and money. So, instead of purchasing or licensing them, the Xerox executives simply went back and copied them.

Just two years after Engelbard's presentation, Xerox was already making substantial progress on their own version of a GUI and mouse, which they were now developing at Xerox PARC, their new research and development facility. The Xerox PARC business plan consisted of developing innovative prototypes and then licensing them to large corporations. This type of business model meant that companies from various industries were always coming in and out of Xerox PARC as they sought the next big thing. But it wouldn't be until 1973 that Xerox had finally developed a workable version of Englebard's inventions, a computer they called *Alto*. For the next six years they continued tinkering with their "Xerox Alto," but were never able to get it to the point where they felt they could sell it commercially. It was certainly a significant improvement over Englebard's earlier version, but they still failed to overcome the key challenge that Englebard had faced—the computer was too costly to be personal.

APPLE MEETS ALTO

By the fall of 1979 Apple software engineer Bill Atkinson had heard about the Xerox Alto and visited the company for a demonstration. He was stunned by what he saw and rushed back to Apple to spread the word. Steve was intrigued and rushed over to Xerox to view the demonstration himself. He knew right away that they were on to something, especially when it came to their redesigned version of Englebard's GUI and mouse. He couldn't help but imagine what Lisa would be like if Apple engineers had access to these kinds of technologies. So, he decided to cut a deal with Xerox in which he would give them the right to purchase Apple stock prior to its IPO and, in exchange, they would "lift their kimono" and give key members of the Lisa team two private Alto demonstrations.

Up to this point Lisa had primarily been in the design stage with improvements to the Apple II, its big moneymaker, still the priority. But in December of 1979 a few Apple execs that included Steve, Bill Atkinson, Bruce Daniels, me, and a few key members of the Lisa team, made the trip to Xerox PARC and were given the demonstration. We were blown away because this was the first computer that we had ever seen that featured a fully workable GUI and mouse. We were in awe of what the Alto could do even if it was too large for practical use and limited in its applications. Just as Xerox executives had been inspired by the Mother of all Demos a decade earlier, we were now similarly inspired to implement our own revolutionary version of Englebard's inventions as part of the Lisa.

Upon my return to Apple, I couldn't stop thinking about the possibilities of what we could do with the things we had just witnessed. Steve and I began conversations about how GUIs were the future of personal computers. We knew that this was exactly what Lisa needed in order to become revolutionary. We all agreed that it was time to move away from traditional text-based, command line operating systems and toward graphical ones that would allow users to interact with computers in all new ways. Not long after that visit, Apple paid Xerox $100,000 for an unlimited license allowing us to utilize Alto technology.

EARLY CHALLENGES

As 1980 rolled around we knew it was going to be a big year for Apple. I spent much of that January having conversations with Steve and others about what the Lisa needed to look like in terms of both software and hardware. We were excited about the idea of designing and developing our own GUI, but we had several challenges that needed to be overcome for this to happen. One of my most immediate challenges was dealing with Lisa's hardware engineer, Ken Rothmuller, who was still arguing that we needed to use function keys, brushing off my insistence that they were no longer needed. By now Steve and I were fully committed to going with a GUI interface and had no intention of reverting back to what we now saw as outdated features. But Ken either didn't get it, or wouldn't accept it, which led me to begin the search for alternative hardware solutions on my own. I simply refused to watch Lisa's software-oriented operating system and applications fail because its hardware couldn't support its functionality.

I could just picture Steve in the Lotus position on our conference table inspecting a Lisa and then calling it a "piece of shit." There was no way I was going to let that happen. But the Ken situation was frustrating because I knew that it would eventually lead to him being fired, which I didn't want to see happen. Steve had already been insisting that I let Ken go, but even if I had wanted to, I couldn't have because I was the VP of Software and Lisa's hardware team did not report to me. In fact, Ken reported directly to Tom Whitney, who felt that he was a key member of his team and did not want to lose him. So, for the time being, Ken and I just had to agree to disagree.

Another early challenge we faced was finding a processor that would be able to power Lisa's GUI. At some point I recalled that in September of the previous year, Motorola's semiconductor department had announced the forthcoming release of the Motorola 68000, the first widely produced 16/32-bit microprocessor, which was twice as powerful as the typical 16-bit microprocessors that had been introduced just six months earlier. The new processor would reportedly be able to support high resolution bitmap displays as well as the interactive user interface we needed to run Lisa's operating system. The Motorola 68000 being released right after our visit to Xerox PARC was either fate or just a happy coincidence.

As promising as this development was, it did not come without its downsides and for us the biggest was the cost. The Motorola 68000 was very expensive and if there was one thing Steve didn't like it was overpaying for anything. This meant I had to successfully make the case to him as to why the Lisa *had* to have this particular chip in order to become the computer of the future that he and I had envisioned. I listed all of the reasons, but it wasn't until I told him it supported virtual memory and that Hitachi would be a second source that relented. For the first time since joining Apple, I finally knew what Lisa's hardware and software needed to look like and what needed to be done in order to begin the development.

MIKE SCOTT

When most people think about Apple leadership the first name that naturally comes to mind is Steve Jobs. What many people don't realize is that while Steve had always been our unofficial leader, and an active co-founder, he was not *technically* Apple's leader. Steve would not take on the CEO role at Apple until his return in 1997, over twenty years after the company was founded. When I started, the person officially listed as CEO was Michael Scott, but we all just called him Scotty. The company was growing so fast, and Steve was so young and had such little business experience that Apple's board of directors believed they needed a proverbial "adult in the room." Apple's other co-founder, Steve Wozniak, was older and more mature, but he was never really an option because he was much more interested in building things than in managing people. This led board member Mike Markkula to take matters into his own hands and recruit Scotty to join Apple as the company's first CEO.

In those days the leadership arrangement was a bit awkward at times, not just because Steve was the co-founder and brains behind Apple, but also because he was the public face of the company and was highly charismatic. Many Apple employees considered Steve to be the real "boss" and his product decisions as being the final word. Scotty was liked and respected but never seemed able to get out from under Steve's long shadow and always seemed too quiet and reserved for that to ever change. Thus, it came as a shock to all of us when, on Friday, February 1, 1980, just three months before the introduction of the Apple III, Scotty decided to put his foot down and, seemingly overnight, make a major decision. His epiphany was that Apple employees needed to get a better understanding of how businesses would utilize the Apple III as a word processor, while also setting an example. So that morning he fired off the following, now notorious, company-wide memo:

<u>YOU ALL BETTER READ THIS</u>

Date: February 1, 1980

To: Purchasing and Everyone

From: Mike Scott

Subject: Typewriters

<u>Effective Immediately!! No more typewriters are to be purchased, leased, etc., etc.</u>

Apple is an innovative company. We must believe and lead in all areas. If word processing is so neat, then let's all use it!

Goal: By 1-1-81 No typewriters at Apple. (Ken, get rid of the DEC word processor ASAP)

Brownie Points: Typewriter users giving up their machines in favor of Apple II-Apple Writer Systems will get first priority on <u>new</u> Apple high performance systems. Those who can justify direct typing capabilities and will turn in their typewriter will get first Qume with Keyboard/ Apple installations.

We believe the typewriter is obsolete. Let's prove it inside before we try and convince our customers.

Cc: Executive Staff
All Typewriter Users

In other words, from that point forward we were going to be required to "eat our own dog food," even though typewriters were still considered to be an absolute necessity for any size business. There was likely not another company in the United States in 1980, much less a fast-growing one, that didn't completely rely on them. All of us at Apple immediately saw that Scotty's sudden directive was a really big deal, especially considering that the Apple III still had hardware issues and that Lisa wasn't being released for another three years!

CHAPTER 4

BUSY TIMES

*"What I'm best at is finding a group of talented
people and making things with them."*

—STEVE JOBS

In the early 1980s Apple was designing, developing, and shipping many new products. The Apple II was still selling well, especially now that it was running the highly anticipated Visi-Calc spreadsheet software. Adding VisiCalc to the Apple II was game-changing as there had never before been spreadsheet software capable of running on a personal computer. Up until this point a microcomputer, like the Apple II, was often thought of as little more than an interesting invention for computer enthusiasts and gamers, but now, with VisiCalc, the business world began to pay attention. For six years in a row the Apple II would become the best-selling personal computer in the world, eclipsing the Apple III, Lisa, Windows-based PCs, and even Macintosh during its first few years. We were finally proving to application developers just how much of a sales impact a single application could make. Years later I would see this phenomenon in action again when I became an initial investor in PageMaker, the first key application for Macintosh.

APPLE III

With Apple now fully committed to using a graphical user interface, Lisa headed into the development phase with the goal of leading our entry into the corporate office market. Meanwhile, the Apple III was still slated to be our primary product for the small business market by achieving these top three goals:

1. to provide a true typewriter-style keyboard with lower- and upper-case letters and an 80-character display,
2. to meet FCC requirements for the business market; and
3. to implement a new operating system and file system to attract additional high-level languages.

Steve had originally planned for the Apple III to be finished in ten months but it ended up taking its engineers two years as problems persisted throughout development. It was finally introduced to the world on May 19, 1980 at the National Computer Conference (NCC) in Anaheim, California. This was Apple's first time attending NCC. In a way that was a good thing, because people in technology are always looking for the next big computer, which is what many at Apple believed we were launching.

There were also drawbacks as a newcomer at NCC, including the poor floor space given to set up booths. Priority booth placements at conferences like these are typically based on longevity, which meant that the longer a company had been paying for trade show space, the better their spot will be on the floor. In this instance, given that IBM had been a staple at NCC for years, they were given front and center placement, meaning just by walking in the building people would come face to face with "Big Blue." But since this was Apple's first time there, our placement ended up being so bad that we weren't even on the main floor. Instead, we had to set up in a nearby annex building, a place that most conferencegoers didn't even know existed.

We knew in advance that our placement at the NCC was going to be bad and that this would severely hinder our ability to reach guests. Given that, Steve, myself, and a few other executives would meet to discuss potential ways to increase our visibility. Many ideas were tossed around, mostly ones that would have cost us a lot of money, but I instinctively thought back to the Banners of Innovation I had created for Apple University and suggested that we needed to throw *creativity* at a problem rather than money.

During one of these brainstorming meetings, I recalled that my dad had once worked for Bourns Electronics, a company that would regularly rent Disneyland for an entire evening for its employees. I suggested to Steve that we could do something similar by renting an evening at Disneyland, offer free tickets, and publish a guide map in the *NCC Daily Comdex* newspaper. The map could have a line of arrows that guests could follow that would lead from the entrance of the building, away from IBM, down the hall, out the door, and directly to our booth in the annex. Steve loved the idea and the plan worked perfectly. Apple ended up having more guests visit our booth than many of the booths that were set up on the main floor. Even John Young, President of Hewlett-Packard, found his way to us to collect Disneyland tickets for his family!

Two months after its introduction, the Apple III was supposed to be shipping, but continued problems with production and internal conflicts pushed the date back to September. When it finally did ship, the problems had proven too much and hindered its success. One of the problems was that only three software programs were available to run on it, even though it had been months since it was introduced. The hardware also had faulty connectors that would cause the motherboard to overheat and the computer to fail. There was also a required rework of 14,000 units on the assembly line, which impacted its availability and success. After all was said and done only 120,000 Apple IIIs were sold until it was officially discontinued in April 1984. It is now considered to be Apple's first product failure.

Throughout the time the Apple III was struggling, the Apple II continued to sell well, and Lisa was progressing in development. But there was also a fourth, lesser-known computer that was still in the research stage. Throughout 1979 and 1980 Jef Raskin and his small publishing team were trying to design a low-cost consumer product. He had tried to get Apple's leadership to take his effort seriously and dedicate more resources toward it, but because Jef had made very little progress, even in the design stage, the project was nearly terminated several times. Each time Jef would plead his case to Scotty and Mike Markkula and was always given an extension. In hindsight, I realize the reason most of us knew so little about Jef's project was because, like Lisa when I first arrived, it was just an idea.

MAKING MOVES

In the summer of 1980, I had the honor of meeting Seymour Papert, a pioneer in the constructionist movement in education, and later in artificial intelligence. I met him at MIT during the early software design phase of Lisa and was given a copy of his LOGO programming language for my then-six-year-old son, Kris. It was created to be a computerized means for improving the way children think and solve problems, and when

I showed it to Kris, I was able to demonstrate how to draw a box by specifying the four corner coordinates. Totally unamazed, he asked, "Why can't I just draw it?" Now I'm not saying my six-year-old impacted the future design of our LisaDraw application, but it certainly didn't go against our thinking.

As I continued working toward meeting my applications directive, I reached out to three former Hewlett-Packard co-workers of mine, Fred Gibbons, Janelle Vedke and John Page and suggested that they should consider forming their own application software firm. I told them there was a lot more money to be made in writing apps for a million Apple IIs than there was for writing software for nine hundred HP 3000 minicomputers. I must have been persuasive, because soon after speaking with them, the trio left HP and co-founded Software Publishing Company (SPC), an application publishing business that specifically targeted the emerging personal computer market.

In a relatively short amount of time, SPC developed multiple applications which included: pfs: "Personal Filing System," an office suite series for the Apple II that provided pfs:Write (a word processor), psf:Plan (a spreadsheet), psf:Report (a report writer) and psf:Graph (business graphic software). These applications became popular, mostly due to their ease-of-use by new computer users. While Apple was never in the startup incubation business, thanks to the arrangement we had with SPC, it took only a few years before they grew into the ninth-largest microcomputer software company in the world.

SOFTWARE HERO

Probably my best and most critical hire as VP of Software came in September of 1980 when I recruited an engineering manager, Wayne Rosing, a superb engineer from Boston's Digital Equipment Corporation (DEC). Wayne never actually applied for the job, but I had heard that he wasn't happy after DEC management suddenly canceled his "Personal DEC" project. Knowing this, I thought that this would be my best chance to convince him to join me at Apple. I cold-called him and when I got him on the phone, I dropped a cliffhanger: "You are not going to believe what Apple is building," I said. "I can't even tell you anything about it over the phone." That got his attention. When he came by and saw what we were doing with Lisa and the GUI he said, "Holy shit!" and instantly agreed to become Lisa's engineering manager.

Much later, after I left Apple the first time, Wayne ended up replacing me as general manager and would eventually go on to Sun Microsystems before becoming Google's first vice president of engineering. I considered myself to have a pretty good eye for talented engineers and if there was one thing, other than having Steve as our leader, that helped ensure Apple's success it was the number of extremely talented people we were able to recruit. This was why, by the end of that September, Apple was able to surpass the $100 million sales mark in just our fourth year, and by our fifth year we had become the fastest-growing company in history. We also hit a smaller, more personal milestone for me reaching a million dollars per month in software sales. Although I attribute that success to my team as a whole, I was honored that Apple presented me with a bronze plaque attached to a wooden clock with the inscription:

John Couch
Software Hero

Faster than a microprocessor, more inspirational than the corporate objectives, Able to leap compiler theory in a single bound.

In appreciation for the energy and vision that led us to our first million-dollar month in software sales.

Apple Computer, Inc.
September 1980

APPLE'S IPO

Apple went public on December 12, 1980. Its initial public stock offering sold 4.6 million shares of the company at $22 per share and by the end of 2018 the stock would be worth ten times that amount. After the IPO everyone at Apple was ecstatic and many of us had even become millionaires. The high risk I took in joining Steve at Apple had led to high reward. Thinking long-term (accepting Apple stock options) over short-term (keeping my higher salary at HP) was by far the better financial decision.

Days after the IPO our investment bank, Goldman Sachs, threw a dinner for the Apple executive team, and so much alcohol was poured that we ended up making an alcohol-fueled commitment that we were all going to bond by running together in the upcoming Bay to Breakers, a 6.5-mile race in San Francisco that stretched from the bay to the ocean. The most interesting thing about this race was that those who ran it often wore some *really* strange garb. Some dressed like dragons, witches, and various cartoon characters, while some chose to run in it without clothes at all!

The day after the Goldman Sachs party it looked like the bond we had created the previous night wasn't just the alcohol talking because Steve and I began to actually train in the Los Gatos hills in preparation to run the race! But when the day of the race came, the only two execs who ended up running in it were myself and Chief Financial Officer Joe Graziano. The most memorable moment for me came when I beat my younger brother in a sprint to the finish line!

DAD'S PROBLEM

By January of 1981 my parents had been running a family business for years, with my mom being a franchisee of a women's health club. My dad had been complaining for years about how difficult it was for him to manage the health club memberships, because he had no way of knowing when they would expire. He also wasn't able to track the ways in which members were finding the club, whether it was through a referral, advertising, or my mom's sales efforts.

I asked him once if he had ever considered creating an application on a computer that could track these things for him. He looked at me like I was crazy, shook his head, and explained that not only did he not have time to sit down and learn how to write computer programs, the only thing he *did* know about computers was that they were too complicated for neophytes to use. He had a point. Back then there wasn't anything like VisiCalc yet and the only thing a novice computer user would see when they turned on their computers was that cold black screen with white text waiting for a command that looked like Martian gibberish to most people.

I told my dad I'd help him by creating an application that would track everything he needed to properly manage mom's club. We drove down to our local Radio Shack, a now defunct electronics store, and bought a basic TRS-80 desktop microcomputer, which was affectionally referred to as the "Trash-80." The computer was a generic Radio Shack model that had been around since 1977 and was less expensive than the Apple II. It wasn't very powerful, but it would be enough for me to write a quick application. After returning home with the computer, we opened the box in the living room and suddenly a gigantic cockroach ran out. My mom freaked out as we continued removing the computer from the box. "No way!" she snapped. "Get that trash out of my living room!" It was called the Trash-80 for good reason.

My dad and I ultimately took the "Trash" out to the garage, where I wrote a basic program for him to monitor the club's memberships. Everything went well with the program at first, but every time I returned home for holidays, I would end up back in the garage adding new features that my dad now needed. The changes were easy for me, but I realized for non-programmers it was confusing and often overwhelming. I knew what was needed was a way for my dad to be able to define his data, and the relationships between that data, without having to rely on a complicated, procedure-oriented language. I also couldn't help thinking about how a graphical user interface, along with applications like VisiCalc, would make a big difference. While Lisa's GUI wasn't yet finished, I did get my dad VisiCalc, which he was able to pick up quickly. The experience showed just how much an easy-to-use application was needed.

Unfortunately, the help I gave my dad came too late, because a few months later the health club franchise went bust. The good news was that my dad was able to see just how much he could do on VisiCalc, which started his love for computers. He became so intrigued by them that he even decided to open his own computer retail store in a nearby shopping center. I asked one of our board members, Mike Markkula, if it would be okay for my dad to sell Apple products in his store. Mike agreed and with that my dad became the owner of Computer Kingdom, which ended up getting quite a bit of business. Not bad considering only a few months earlier my dad had been so frustrated by the overall complexity of computers.

My mom loves to tell the story about how Steve Jobs and Steve Wozniak had pulled up to Computer Kingdom's grand opening in a big black limousine. When they got out, she recalls, Steve patted his pockets, looked at her and said, "Woz and I don't have any money. Would you mind tipping the driver?" Of course, this was only months after Apple's IPO when they both had a net worth of over $400 million! Steve also got a kick out of the custom license plate on my mom's car that read "BuyAppl." It was arguably the best advice ever written on a license plate.

BLACK WEDNESDAY

On the morning of February 25, 1981, one year after Scotty had sent out his company-wide "No More Typewriters" memo, he felt it was once again time to shake things up, so around 9 AM he began summoning employees, one at a time, to his office. Apple's IPO was still fresh on everyone's mind and things seemed to be going well, but Scotty clearly didn't agree. By 10:30 AM he had fired over thirty Apple employees, including half of the Apple II/III engineers and even their managers. The morning was slow and painful for many of our employees, because no one knew who would be called next.

Being VP of Software I was not a target of his mass firings, but I was very concerned about the impact this would have on Apple's culture. Steve was too busy with his projects to pay attention to what was happening, and Woz was recovering from a debilitating plane accident that had occurred two weeks prior. Around 11 AM Scotty sent a message to Apple survivors that there would be a meeting in Taco Towers at noon. During the meeting he told us that he felt many employees had become "too complacent" and that the big shake-up he was doing was a necessity. That dark day at Apple would soon become referred to as Black Wednesday.

Andy Herzfeld, a prominent member of Apple's design team, noted that just prior to Black Wednesday Scotty had sought the approval of ACM and the rest of the board to go forward with the firings, but after not hearing back from them he went ahead anyway. The board was furious when they learned of the Black Wednesday massacre. This was especially true for ACM, the one who had hired Scotty as CEO in the first place. But Scotty was not fired, which must have emboldened him even more, because he was not done shaking things up. At some point, during the two weeks after Black Wednesday, he decided the entire Apple organizational structure needed a redesign and took it upon himself to plan and execute the largest organizational change the company had ever faced.

CHAPTER 5

LISA

*"I want to build really good tools that I
know in my gut and my heart will be valuable."*

—STEVE JOBS

Black Wednesday shocked all of us, but especially our engineers. Apple's organization had always operated under dedicated functions: hardware, software, marketing, sales, finance, and operations/manufacturing. While our early manufacturing and engineering teams had never seen things completely eye to eye, the mass firings and the challenges of the Apple III had caused a larger rift than usual. As their differences heated up, Tom Whitney, our head of engineering, decided to take a vacation and left for Europe, which thrust Scotty into the role of referee between our manufacturing and engineering teams, each blaming the other for the Apple III delays.

Scotty was upset that Tom had left these difficult decisions up to him. In an effort to rectify these departmental differences, Scotty called an executive meeting in March of 1981, saying he had a "big announcement." It had been less than a month since his Black Wednesday shake-up, so we were all a bit on edge about what he was going to do this time. Many thought we were in for more firings, but Scotty had something bigger in mind.

Seemingly out of nowhere he had made the unilateral decision to realign Apple's entire organizational structure. "From this point forward," he told us, "we'll no longer be organized according to functional units, but instead by product-based *divisions*." This was a huge change that completely caught us off-guard. "One general manager will now oversee a single product line and will be responsible and accountable for all of the development, marketing, engineering and pilot manufacturing for that specific product." We looked around at one another, unsure what to make of this bombshell. Not only was Scotty implementing a fundamental change to Apple's product development, marketing, sales and manufacturing efforts, but he had also chosen who would be the general manager of each division.

Gene Carter was put in charge of the "Personal Computer Systems" division, which included the Apple II and Apple III product lines. Tom Vernard would be running a "Peripherals Division," which included printers, disk drives, and the mouse. Carl Carlson would be overseeing our "Operations and High Volume Manufacturing" division. And I was now General Manager and Vice President of Lisa's Personal Office System division. Perhaps the most shocking part of Scotty's overhaul was that he had also given Steve a new role, giving him the title of "Chairman of the Board." It may have sounded good but in reality, it meant that Steve would no longer have an operational role and he was not pleased.

GENERAL MANAGER

Under Scotty's new organization, I was essentially being promoted from VP of Software to General Manager overseeing the entire Lisa division. After the meeting Steve approached Scotty and told him that he wanted to be in charge of the Lisa project, but Scotty felt he wasn't ready to manage and operate an entire division and denied his request. Steve then lobbied Gene Carter and Mike Markkula, both of whom backed Scotty's decision to leave the Lisa division under my direction. Steve was highly disappointed, and I had mixed feelings on the matter. On one hand I was excited about the new responsibility I was given, but I also knew that Steve was the creative visionary *and* company founder who could have easily used his powers of persuasion to ensure Lisa's success. I wondered if there might be a way for him to run Lisa but have the rest of the team report to me, similar to the way it had been in our New Products group but I was told that wasn't an option.

I still think about what might have happened with Lisa (and Macintosh) had Scotty put Steve in charge of Lisa and I worked for him. Would Lisa have gotten the respect and resources it later lacked? Would Steve have canceled the "personal office system" and focused only on a consumer product to replace the Apple II? Would the Lisa have been the computer that conquered the world? For years I found myself reflecting on this, but eventually came to accept the way it happened, which may have been exactly the approach Apple needed in order to introduce so many new concepts to the world of personal computing.

After Scotty's big shuffle, we learned that, just as with Black Wednesday, the spontaneous reorganization had been done without board approval. Mike Markkula was upset, and this time had seen enough. He removed Scotty as CEO and gave him the powerless position of "Vice Chairman." Mike took over as interim-CEO and a few months later Scotty resigned. Steve had also given up, at least in terms of trying to persuade Mike to let him run Lisa. He still wanted nothing more than to develop a revolutionary Apple computer, but begrudgingly came to accept that it wasn't going to be Lisa. Instead, he started looking around for something else and eventually came upon Jef Raskin's publishing team and the mysterious low-cost project he had been trying to get off the ground for two years. It still wasn't much of a computer yet, but Jef had managed to give it a really cool name—Macintosh.

MACINTOSH

Jef Raskin had been hired in January of 1978 to create a publishing department that would write and publish owner manuals for Apple's computers. But he had bigger aspirations than just writing manuals, he wanted to design and develop his own computer. He made no secret of his ambition to Mike Markkula, to whom he reported directly, and Mike even agreed that he could work on a design but needed to keep him apprised on a weekly basis. Early on Jef was referring to his "forthcoming" computer as Macintosh, but for years he wasn't able to take it very far beyond the idea stage. When I recently spoke to Mike about his first time seeing Jef's Macintosh he recalled, "It was just a cardboard mockup. It had an integrated keyboard and screen, no mouse, and no trackpad."

By the time Steve had found his way to Jef, the Macintosh project still hadn't moved any further in the development process than it had when Markkula had first seen it. Steve boldy began inviting himself to Jef's Macintosh meetings, but was not impressed by what he was seeing. He soon concluded that *he* needed to be the one developing Macintosh and began playing his founder's card to oust Jef from his own project. Once Steve took over Macintosh, he promptly began redesigning it to be a revolutionary computer made for the consumer market, similar to what Lisa was going to be for the corporate market.

Rather than starting from scratch on this, Steve decided to speed things up by leveraging the best ideas of Lisa, while reducing its expensive functionality to better fit what he believed a *personal* computer needed. He even announced to his new team that the Macintosh was going to be a "more affordable, more accessible, consumer version of Lisa." I loved the idea and didn't view it as a competition, because we were targeting two different markets. I knew it would be good strategy to leverage Lisa's application software, adapt it for Macintosh, and let users run the same applications at home on a Mac that they did at work on a Lisa.

Much has been made by the media about Steve supposedly being "kicked off of the Lisa team" and how he held a grudge when developing the Macintosh, but neither is true. While he was no longer *directly* involved in Lisa's development, we both shared a vision and strategic direction, and as Apple's co-founder, VP of New Products, and now chairman, he played an important role right from the start. It's true that Steve was disappointed about not being allowed to oversee Lisa, but I never felt he held a grudge against me or my team. Throughout the development process of both computers, he and I continued to talk and share information and resources, including transferring experienced Lisa programmers to the Mac team. But we were also still highly competitive.

THE BET

On April 20, 1981 Steve and I made a private bet. While my Lisa team was knee-deep in the development process, and the Macintosh team was ankle-deep in theirs, we agreed to wager $5,000 (although we would later change it from dollars to a dinner) on which of our computers would ship first. The idea for the bet arose from conversations he and I had about ways to further motivate our respective teams. Apple was full of Type-A, competitive people and we knew that framing the bet as a competition between teams would act to motivate them to work harder to meet challenging deadlines. The plan worked well, but at some point, it began working a bit *too* well. Steve's Macintosh team started taking the friendly competition much more seriously than my Lisa team. For the Mac team it became all about "Let's beat those high-level language, computer-science master's degree guys over in Lisa, with our hackers and assembly coding forte," and they began to really increase their speed. Suddenly, I watched as important resources got redirected from Lisa to Macintosh. The worst part came when several of my key team members were recruited by Steve and persuaded to leave my Lisa team and join him on the Mac. It was a difficult situation for me, but Steve was one of our founders and the face of Apple so there was nothing I could do about it. To my delight though, Lisa did end up shipping a full year before Macintosh, which prompted Steve to throw my Lisa team an amazing celebratory party—with a giant mock-up check for $5,000.

Meanwhile, as his Mac team got further along in development, Steve realized that they wouldn't have to build a development environment, because they had the ability to leverage Lisa's development environment to code in a high-level language. That way, he figured, he could just go out and buy applications rather than having to create them from scratch like we had to do for Lisa. It was this thinking that would eventually lead him to make his infamous "deal of the century" with Bill Gates, sparking a corporate competition that would last decades. But for now, the only competition Apple had so far was internal. That was about to change.

WELCOME, IBM. SERIOUSLY.

As Lisa and Macintosh continued their rapid pace development, the media began hearing whispers about a couple of "revolutionary computers" that Apple was working on, but they hadn't yet gotten enough information to report it. It wasn't until the fall of 1981 that they finally had *something* to talk about—IBM had suddenly become Apple's biggest competitor.

"Big Blue," as IBM was often called, had for years been the most dominant company in the computer mainframe business, but had now decided to sell personal computers as well. So, to much fanfare, they released the IBM Personal Computer (IBM PC), an open system allowing users to replace both internal and external components with third-party ones so long as they were "IBM compatible." Steve bought one of the IBM PCs and tested it out. He looked over its hardware and software and then, in true Steve fashion, proclaimed that the entire thing was an absolute "piece of shit."

He was right, because the IBM PC's parts and overall quality weren't even close to what we were working with on Lisa, which was a big relief to me. But this was the moment that would mark the beginning of a decades-long debate on whether customizable, open systems (like PCs) or more reliable, closed systems (like Macs) were better. It's a debate that continues today and not just around hardware. On the software side the same open versus closed debate involves operating systems (Windows versus MacOS) and mobile phones (Android versus iOS). There is no right or wrong answer as to which type of systems are better because what it ultimately comes down to is what the user values more, customization or reliability.

Prior to IBM launching their own personal computers, Apple had few competitive worries. But IBM was a household name that everyone knew and that forced us to act. IBM had been promoting their PC primarily in trade magazines and newspapers and we were concerned that corporate businesses might choose them over Apple simply due to brand recognition. There was even a popular saying in the mainframe world,

"No one ever lost their job for choosing IBM!" Despite the concerns, Steve was thrilled that IBM had entered the game, because he understood that they would end up validating the existence of the personal computer market, which had not yet been established or taken seriously by the general public. Just as IBM's PC fanfare began really heating up, Steve ran a full-page ad in *The Wall Street Journal* that read:

Welcome, IBM. Seriously.

Welcome to the most exciting and important marketplace since the computer revolution began 35 years ago.

And congratulations on your first personal computer.

Putting real computer power in the hands of the individual is already improving the way people work, think, learn, communicate and spend their leisure hours.

Computer literacy is fast becoming as fundamental a skill as reading and writing.

When we invented the first personal computer system, we estimated that over 140,000,000 people worldwide could justify the purchase of one, if only they understood its benefits.

Next year alone, we project that well over 1,000,000 will come to that understanding. Over the next decade, the growth of the personal computer will continue in logarithmic leaps.

We look forward to responsible competition in the massive effort to distribute this American technology to the world.

And we appreciate the magnitude of your commitment.

Because what we are doing is increasing social capital by enhancing individual productivity.

Welcome to the task.
—Apple

The self-promoting, passive-aggressive ad was smart and certainly got the attention of the business world, which now began to view Apple as a legitimate alternative to IBM. Steve felt that having IBM validate the market was significant because it would allow us to position ourselves as being rebels and pirates, while simultaneously positioning IBM as representing a more traditional navy, and everyone knows that it's more fun to be a pirate than to join the navy! Steve would continue to run with the pirate analogy for quite a while and even went so far as to raise a pirate flag above the Macintosh building.

A few years after *The Wall Street Journal* ad, Apple began refocusing its message away from businesses and toward Macintosh's target market, the mainstream public. We ran a brilliant advertising campaign with the now infamous Super Bowl commercial titled, "Why 1984 Won't Be Like 1984," which positioned IBM as the enemy of the people. The ad was based on George Orwell's dystopian novel, *1984*, which focused on technology being used to control people. In dull greys and whites, a large image of "Big Brother" covered the screen, speaking down to a room of cult-like drones about the "Unification of Thoughts" (representing IBM). A colorful woman (representing

Apple) then bolts through the room, chased by state police, and tosses a sledgehammer through the screen, destroying Big Brother. Even though the ad was designed to introduce Macintosh, it was a perfect example of the way in which we had been positioning IBM for years—and it worked.

A SHARED VISION

Transitioning from VP of Software to General Manager gave me total control over every aspect of Lisa, including software and hardware. Overnight, Ken, who was still technically head of Lisa hardware, now worked for me instead of Tom Whitney. Ken had never stopped arguing that Lisa needed to have an Apple-designed, bit-sliced, 16-bit microprocessor rather than the Motorola 68000 that Steve and I had already decided was needed. He was also *still* arguing for the use of traditional function keys rather than relying on a GUI and never aligned himself with the vision for Lisa that Steve and I were working to realize.

Eventually, Steve had heard enough. He called me, frustrated that Ken would not get on board, and insisted that I fire him. I told Tom what Steve said and that I would have to fire Ken if he continued to refuse to get on board, but Tom wasn't able to change his mind either. Ken was a proud man with a traditional mindset, but Apple was a fast-growing company at which tradition was considered the antithesis of innovation. Unfortunately, I was forced to let him go. I lost a hard worker and good friend that day, but it just couldn't be helped. The Apple train was roaring full speed ahead and anyone not on board got left behind.

After Ken's departure, I replaced him with managers who shared the GUI and mouse-driven vision that Steve and I desired for Lisa. On the hardware side key people included Wayne

Rosing, my right-hand man, Ken Okin, his right-hand man, Dan Smith, Robert Paratore, and Bill Dresselhaus. I also brought in a small team from the design studio, IDEO. On the software side key team members included Bruce Daniels, who ran applications, and Larry Tesler, who oversaw system software, Bill Atkinson, Andy Hertfield, Steve Capps, and Chris Franklin. I recruited computer scientists from the best engineering universities, and others from top companies, primarily HP and Xerox PARC. Finally, I hired a team of people from the minicomputer industry that specialized in operating systems. We started off working out of an Apple office known as "Taco Towers" on Stevens Creek Boulevard in Cupertino, but quickly outgrew it and moved to the much larger Bandley 5 building, where together we would bring Lisa to life.

DATAGRAMMING

With the new team in place, we began to more thoroughly clarify our vision for Lisa. Steve and I had always wanted to redefine Lisa's user interface to reflect the GUI we had seen at Xerox PARC. But we had also discussed adding additional applications that would empower the end user to move data from one application to another in a "cut and paste" paradigm. I spent a lot of time trying to figure out how to make it all work. Before I became General Manager, just after becoming VP of Software, I had written an article called "datagramming" that was fundamentally the strategic direction for Apple software. The article compared the common procedure-oriented languages of the day to a different type of software that would be needed in order for non-programmers to share data between applications.

For instance, the software would have to be written in a high-level language, such as Pascal, rather than in assembly code like that used for the Apple II. There also needed to be an environment where users could easily move data between these applications without having to go through the file system. This type of environment would require a powerful processor, which is why Rich Page and I ended up fighting so hard for the Motorola 68000. It would be a year before my datagramming article was actually published, but it would now become my inspiration for Lisa's GUI functionality and help guide our entire software efforts.

At one point during Lisa's development, we had an opportunity to push its hardware out with a traditional vanilla interface by releasing it as a 68000 network workstation. It would have been significant because most personal computers at that time were not 16-bit. The proposed workstation version of Lisa even managed to get a moniker: "Lucy: The Dirty Lisa." To be honest, we probably could have sold a ton of Lucy workstations, especially to universities, because they would have been powerful $5,000 Unix-based machines. But Unix didn't have file protection and we couldn't successfully move into a business environment without being able to protect users' files. More importantly, Lucy wasn't consistent with our vision for Lisa, which had always been to revolutionize *personal* computing. Fortunately, the Lucy idea was abandoned, and we were able to refocus on the real Lisa.

One thing I wanted to make sure of was that, throughout the development process, we kept the end user in mind to ensure that Lisa would be able to gain widespread acceptance. I would always require proof of concept before making major decisions. We frequently tested concepts on real users and use their feedback to make usability adjustments. One thing I did to test our changes was to bring Apple employees in and, without any direction, ask them to try and figure out on their own how to use Lisa. If they could do it in fifteen minutes or less, then we knew we were on the right track. If not, then it was back to the drawing board.

At some point I showed Lisa to Bank of America President Sam Armicost, who stopped me mid-presentation and called his wife. "I need you to come down to the office," he told her. "I want to show you the first computer you'll actually be able to use." It was an encouraging start. Never before had the public been able to use a computer that combined hardware innovations like the mouse with software innovations like a graphical user interface. It was this integrated behavior of both revolutionary hardware *and* software, working seamlessly together, that became known as "Lisa Technology."

CHAPTER 6

LISA TECHNOLOGY

"We're really banking everything on Lisa's technology."

—STEVE JOBS

Lisa Technology was unlike anything the world had ever seen in terms of both hardware and software. On the hardware side it included the Motorola 68000 CPU, clocked at 5 MHz and featuring 1mb of memory upgradeable to 2mb (eight times larger than Macintosh would have on release), an internal 5mb hard disk that allowed for large data files and the ability to store more robust applications on a Sony floppy drive, rather than floppy disks. It was also able to connect via a TCP-IP network, a document file server, and an Oracle server.

Lisa's mouse was an extremely important piece of hardware. It allowed users to easily switch between documents with a simple point and click, although we weren't sure how quickly people would accept the transition from a text-based editor to a mouse. At this juncture mice were unheard of beyond the world of computer geeks, and even among us it was often decried as being a fun device for gaming rather than as a revolutionary tool. Many people swore that no one would ever remove their hand from a keyboard to click on a silly little mouse.

As with our GUI, the final version of our mouse ended up looking nothing like the one we saw on the Xerox Alto. The cursor was smooth with a lightning-fast response time and we played around with the shape and size of it until it was able to fit snugly in the palm of our hand. Our ultimate goal for it was to make it so that computer users could focus entirely on their work and forget that the mouse was even there.

Throughout Lisa's design process there were sometimes differences of opinion between our engineering and marketing teams. One of their most memorable arguments was whether or not users would prefer using a one-button or multi-button mouse. I found the whole thing ridiculous and trivial. I knew that we had something so game-changing that users would be happy to use either one so long as it increased their productivity. "Let's not argue about whether we have diamonds or emeralds," I would tell them, "when the rest of the world has coal." In the end, given Apple's obsession with simplicity, we went with a single button.

The use of keyboards wasn't new, but the way we refashioned Lisa's was unique. One of the more interesting features of it was that it included a collection of small, pull-out help cards with instructions designed to keep users from having to consult bulky user manuals. Blank cards were also installed on the keyboard on which users could make their own notes. Another unique feature was that Lisa's keyboard was able to self-identify the primary language of users and automatically translate diagnostic messages into their native tongue.

A key decision we made for Lisa was to use thumbscrews rather than traditional screws that would have required the use of screwdrivers. The back panel was also removable, allowing for easy access to Lisa's internal components, making it the only Apple computer to date with an open hardware system. Every Apple computer, including the Macintosh, has come as a closed system in which users cannot upgrade individual internal pieces. We wanted to make sure that it was as simple as possible for users to disassemble and upgrade components, another example of our always prioritizing simplicity.

GRAPHICAL USER INTERFACE

I knew that the feature that would make Lisa stand out above every other computer was, by far, our graphical user interface. We had always intended to make a computer that allowed user-friendly integration on multiple tasks, required a minimal amount of training, and would be easy-to-use. But we also recognized that trying to get anything revolutionary to be accepted by mainstream users is never an easy task. It's human nature to be drawn to the familiar over the unfamiliar, which is why we wanted to make Lisa's GUI feel like a digital version of a real-world office. To accomplish this, we built a simple file management system that would give our electronic desktop the appearance of a real desktop.

On top of this digital desktop, we wanted users to be able to view multiple applications at once, drag and drop data with the flick of a mouse, and use a virtual clipboard to copy, edit and paste data across different applications. We also wanted to create a standard look and feel across each application that allowed for new experiences, while maintaining an ever-important air of familiarity. This was why we chose terms like *desktop*, *files* and *folders*, rather than computer jargon, and why we wanted users to be able to click on and drag desktop icons that represented these files and folders. And just as like in a real office, we wanted users to be able to easily open, place, move, rename, and trash files.

Our first attempt at creating this digital desktop interface was called the *Filer*. Once Lisa was booted up, the software asked the user questions in order to determine the task they wanted to accomplish and then automatically execute the appropriate function needed to start it. While the software was unique and powerful, our engineering team still wanted to make it more user-friendly. But there was a bit of pushback about doing so, because the head of Marketing was concerned that we wouldn't have time to do it without delaying Lisa's release. But Bill Atkinson and a few others were determined to get a new interface on Lisa and teamed up to make it happen. Over the course of a single weekend, they created *Desktop Manager*, a brand-new interface that acted both as a file organizer *and* a program manager. When they showed it off the following Monday, we were blown away and knew instantly that we had a winner.

LISA SOFTWARE

When all was said and done, the amount of pioneering software that was included with Lisa was astonishing. For example, the most important items for computer users back then were programs, not documents. But this meant they needed to know which program to open and then create the appropriate document within that program, which was often confusing.

During Lisa's design process we realized that it was easier when users were able to focus directly on their documents, programs needed to become a means to an end. This led us to make Lisa software *document-centered*, a seemingly small, but highly effective change. Apparently, this had some sticking power too, because even today when we click on a document our computer automatically launches the proper program and we're ready to work.

Lisa also came with a low power feature that was ahead of its time. Back then computers had to be shut down completely and fully rebooted which was always a *very* slow process. But because Lisa's power button relied on software rather than hardware, the computer could be turned on and off quickly. Doing it this way not only saved power, but also saved and restored previous sessions, which included user preferences, open applications and open documents.

Pop-up error messages were especially innovative on Lisa because, unlike error messages today with cryptic text like "System Error 45256," Lisa's pop-up boxes provided detailed summaries of the problem in plain English and even told users exactly how to fix them. They also provided a way for users to run their own diagnostics whenever they wanted through what we called a "Service Mode." We even included the ability for users to customize settings and features in ways that fit their personalized needs and a "Preferences" module where they could adjust the contrast of their monitor, dim the screen, and turn on a screen privacy feature.

Lisa was designed for the office market, meaning that security would be a major concern to users, so we spent quite a bit of time creating ways to improve encryption. Beyond general password protection, we went further and added unique features as well that included protected memory and extreme copy protection, neither of which had been included on any other computer. To do this, we made sure each Lisa had a distinctive, fixed serial number encoded onto its motherboard. Any software purchased on it would be locked into that particular machine, thus completely eliminating the resale of used software. Today's digital rights management (DRM), which links software to a certain account or piece of hardware, is a direct spinoff of that system. There was also document-specific password protection, a feature that many operating systems today still don't provide!

Our graphical user interface made command-line operating systems look like relics from the Stone Age. Lisa was not only the first commercial computer with a GUI and mouse, it introduced dozens of new features that have stood the test of time. While the use of windows, menus, and icons are the most obvious game-changers, other things we introduced heavily influenced later technology as well, such as our Office

Suite, which led to Microsoft Office, and our Desktop Manager, which led to Apple Finder.

What it boils down to is that Lisa Technology, with its synergy between innovative hardware and innovative software, was built for one specific purpose: to make computers user-friendly and easy to use. I believed we did that, and I could not have been prouder of my team. We ended up introducing something to the world that no one had ever seen before and that many people didn't think possible. Even so, we also learned that the road to innovation is never easy. When designing and developing *any* product, much less a revolutionary one, the only thing manufacturers can 100 percent count on is that there will be significant challenges and the work we did on Lisa was no exception. Beyond typical day-to-day issues, we ended up facing three major challenges: Twiggy drives, the price point, and the innovation dilemma.

CHALLENGES: TWIGGY

One of the biggest challenges we faced came from a 5.25 double-sided floppy disk known as "Twiggy." Steve believed in the Twiggy drive and was planning on using it in both Lisa and Macintosh. I was concerned whether or not Apple had the experience and expertise to even build a drive at all and I knew that any single faulty component could ruin an otherwise perfect computer. But I was ultimately overruled on this and, despite my concerns, Lisa shipped with not one, but *two* Twiggy drives. As I predicted, once Lisa was released, the Twiggy drives proved disastrous. Users found that they were too slow, that they often got stuck, and that they sometimes failed to work altogether. The biggest problem with things like this is that when part of a computer malfunctions, users aren't going to blame that specific part, they're going to blame the entire computer.

You won't hear average users say, "This disk drive is a piece of crap!" You're going to hear, "This computer is a piece of crap!" One might even be tempted to make a proverb out of it: "Lisa's Law": If one part of a computer is broken, the whole thing is broken!

It was heartbreaking to hear the frequent complaints related to the faulty Twiggy drive, especially since I suspected there could be problems prior to Lisa's release. Eventually more reliable drives would be added and replace the Twiggy, but by that time Lisa's reputation for reliability had already taken a major blow. In the meantime, Steve watched the negative impact Twiggy was having on Lisa's sales and reputation and began frantically looking at ways to fix the problem. He did so, not just to salvage Lisa, but also because Twiggy drives were set to be included in the Macintosh as well, which was due for release less than a year after Lisa's launch. Some people were trying to convince Steve to abandon Twiggy altogether and start looking for third-party drives. But he felt that Apple had invested a lot in developing the drives and that we should be in no hurry to toss them out and hope something new came along in time for Macintosh's release. And there was no way in the world *that* was going to be delayed.

While Steve was bearing down on the hardware team to quickly fix the Twiggy drives, Sony released a new 3.5" rigid floppy disk. Macintosh's hardware manager realized the potential of this new drive and quietly flew to Sony headquarters in Japan. His plan was to meet with Sony engineers and try to figure out a way that their new drive would work on a Macintosh. Doing this without Steve's knowledge was risky, but with so little time before the Mac's release, something needed to be done quickly, even if it was just having a Plan B.

Not long after that trip to Japan, Sony engineers started showing up at Apple to try and build an interface between their

3.5″ disk drives and the Macintosh. The Mac hardware team, however, had no intention of telling Steve about these visits until they knew for sure it would work. The secrecy was so intense, as the story goes, that whenever Steve would enter the building, the Sony engineers were rounded up and hidden in closets! Whether it was actually that extreme or not, the story made for some interesting watercooler chats.

Once Sony and Apple engineers figured out how to interface the drive and Macintosh, it was shown to Steve. Despite his preference for internal hardware development, he was impressed by the smaller, sexier unit and how much more reliable the Sony disk drives were compared to the Twiggy, and he agreed to include them in Macs. If only they had been available to Lisa, it would have been one less challenge for us to overcome.

CHALLENGES: PRICE POINTS

A second major challenge prior to Lisa's release was price. We knew going in that Lisa was going to be priced higher than usual in order to recoup some of our development expenses. What we didn't know was that it was going to be listed for a whopping $10,000. It was far more than anything Apple had ever sold, and instantly made Lisa the most expensive microcomputer in the world. In 1983 dollars, $10,000 is equivalent to $26,000 in 2020, and that was *per computer*. Such an extreme price tag made Lisa unaffordable to the vast majority of potential buyers. Research done after Lisa's release showed that its price point was the single biggest reason for it not having the market success we had hoped for.

Another key issue, which started much earlier in the development process, was leaks. As far back as the summer of 1982 I remember Steve being extremely excited about Lisa's graphical user interface. He sometimes couldn't hold back his excitement and began sneaking hints to the press, long before its introduction and corresponding press tour. As I often say, it's a strange ship that leaks from the top! The early development leaks were somewhat painful, but not nearly as bad as the one that happened in late 1982, just prior to Lisa's introduction.

Steve did continue to talk to the press about Lisa, but not in the way I had hoped. Now, whenever he did an interview on it, he would also mention a *second* computer Apple was in the process of developing. One that not only had a graphical user interface and mouse like Lisa, the best thing about it, he noted, was that it was going to be sold *at a fraction of the price!* It seemed to me as though the Macintosh leaks were far more devastating than the Lisa leaks when it came to its ultimate success. It was obvious to me that not many people would want to buy a $10,000 computer when they could wait a bit longer for a $2,500 one that apparently had all the same functionality! The strange ship that leaked from the top had begun sinking before ever leaving the dock!

CHALLENGES: INNOVATION DILEMMA

Another major challenge we faced with Lisa was the lack of available software applications upon its release, which came from a conundrum we found ourselves in that I refer to as an innovation dilemma. A key strategy in the success of the Apple II had been our ability to rely on third-party software. Recall that one of my primary objectives as VP of Software had been to realize Steve's vision of ensuring that "every application in the world be able to run on Apple II." I knew that an open system was the only way to do that, and it worked because there were a lot of developers who could write programs in assembly code, which the Apple II required until later, when we released the Pascal and Fortran languages.

Lisa's operating system and graphical user interface, on the other hand, was written in Pascal, and the GUI environment was *so* new that hardly anyone outside of our team knew how to program in it. We had found ourselves in a Catch-22. We needed to provide programmers with reliable APIs (Application Programming Interfaces), but we first needed to learn how to develop in a GUI environment ourselves.

By being so revolutionary we had placed ourselves into an innovation dilemma. This severely limited the number of third-party applications we would be able to include in Lisa upon its release. Obviously shipping a computer with no applications preloaded, no way to buy them, and no way to create them, would have been ridiculous. So, we had to quickly write *all* of Lisa's initial applications in-house while simultaneously designing the application interfaces (APIs) for third-party programmers. That meant the guidelines and tools for writing software for Lisa would not be available at introduction. However, it *was* available to the Macintosh team, allowing them to program their own applications on Lisa and then download the software to run on the Mac.

What we ended up creating, given such a short amount of time, was the *Lisa Office System*, a bundled office suite consisting of seven key applications: LisaWrite, LisaCalc, LisaDraw, LisaGraph, LisaProject, LisaList, and LisaTerminal. Each application was designed so people could use a computer to do work that previously needed to be done on paper. It was the first office suite that had ever been bundled together and served as the precursor to Macintosh's Office Suite and eventually to Microsoft Office. I was proud of the work we did in creating Lisa's Office Suite but would have loved to have had time to secure more applications that could have been pre-installed prior to shipping.

We were later able to open up our desktop libraries to outside developers through a tool we created called the *Lisa*

ToolKit. The libraries consisted of dozens of software modules used by in-house Lisa applications, including Bill Atkinson's *QuickDraw*, a powerful graphics module. Fortunately, we had ensured that Lisa's environment window allowed users to boot the computer in more than one user mode. The primary mode for non-technical users was through the GUI, which also gave them access to the Office Suite. Later we added another user mode through which developers could access a second operating system that featured a text-based GUI editor called *Lisa Workshop* (later refashioned as the *Lisa Monitor* environment). It was a workable development environment, but not an ideal one because developers had to physically reboot their computer every time they needed to switch operating systems. What we needed was an environment in which outside developers could create software *within* Lisa's Office System itself, but again, given the time constraints, the way we ended up doing it was our only option.

CORPORATE JEWELS

At one point during the 1982 development process of both Lisa and Macintosh, Steve attempted to solve our innovation dilemma by reaching out to a fast-rising software developer named Bill Gates. Bill was CEO of Microsoft, a Bellevue, Washington-based software company that he and his partner, Paul Allen, had founded. The company had entered the operating system business a few years earlier and by 1981 had released a command-line operating system called MS-DOS. A year earlier Bill had negotiated a contract with IBM to develop an operating system for the IBM PC. It was a major deal for Microsoft, pushing the small software company into a period of rapid growth.

Steve was impressed by Microsoft's sudden success and came up with a plan. Rather than leverage our Lisa Office Suite applications, he was going to convince Bill to have Microsoft develop spreadsheet and word processing applications specifically for Macintosh. While I had been fighting for Apple to allow third-party developers to write applications for our computers, I wasn't thrilled with the idea of hiring one that was also in the operating system business, and especially Bill Gates, who was already gaining a reputation as a shrewd opportunist.

I tried to talk Steve out of the idea, but he didn't listen and flew to Microsoft headquarters to pitch his idea directly to Bill. I knew Steve was more of a visionary, but Bill was a cunning businessman who could sniff out opportunity a mile away. He agreed to Steve's proposal without a second thought. When Steve returned, he boasted about the deal to the executive staff saying, "I just made the greatest deal in the history of mankind!" The deal, he explained, was that Microsoft would write word processor and spreadsheet applications for Macintosh for only a $1 royalty per application. Steve was absolutely ecstatic.

While the deal may have sounded good to Steve at the time, it didn't take me long to realize the ramifications of what just happened. Macintosh did not yet have its own development environment, meaning Microsoft would not be able to utilize it to write the applications. In fact, all Macintosh software was still being written on Lisa and then ported over. This meant that in order for Microsoft to write programs for Macintosh they would need to do it on *Lisa*. After the executive meeting I pulled Steve aside. "Steve, you just sold the corporate jewels," I told him. "Because now we have to give Bill Gates access to Lisa Technology!"

MICROSOFT

By late 1982, Apple's "ship that leaks from the top" had flooded. The media and just about everyone on earth knew that we were on the verge of launching a revolutionary computer and we began getting inundated by requests to view it. We didn't feel as though this was a bad thing because, yes, we wanted to give potential corporate customers a perspective beyond that of the Apple II, and yes, we wanted them to see how much better our product was than the IBM PC. To make this happen, Trip Hawkins' marketing team guided us in designing and building a special "Sneak Preview" room where Lisa could be viewed in a private setting. Today such rooms at Apple are referred to as executive "briefing centers."

Inside the Sneak Preview room were six Lisas, each running different applications. Our sales department had invited Fortune 400 companies in to witness the future of personal computing. No one had ever seen anything like Lisa, and those who did see it were blown away. One of those people was Bill Gates, who had flown down to see it firsthand. As instructed by Steve, I proceeded to give Bill a full demonstration of all the things Lisa could do. Bill and I went from one machine to another. "How'd you do that?" he asked. "You're going too fast. Show me that again!" He was like a kid in a candy store. I could practically hear his mind churning during his entire visit.

After the demonstration, Bill headed back to Seattle and I was directed to ship him two of our pre-release Lisas so that his team could begin working on the Macintosh applications. As much as I hated to do it, the directive came from Steve himself, so I really had no choice.

As promised, Bill did go on to write the applications for Macintosh, but also ended up doing a lot more than that. In a savvy, somewhat unethical, move he instructed his Microsoft team to leverage Lisa Technology, primarily our graphical user interface, and begin developing their own *very* similar GUI with the idea of using it to replace their DOS-based system. Bill would go on to call his "new" GUI software Microsoft Windows.

It was a slap in Apple's face that Microsoft would essentially copy Lisa's GUI feature by feature, but Bill didn't stop there. He also released the *Microsoft Mouse*, which "coincidentally" was *very* similar to Lisa's mouse and, to make matters worse, in 1983, the exact same year Lisa was released with our pre-installed Office Suite, Microsoft released its own, *very* similar, office suite called *Microsoft Office*, which included *Microsoft Excel* and *Microsoft Word*. Unfortunately, when I had told Steve he had "sold the corporate jewels," I was right.

Years after the Microsoft debacle, John Sculley, Apple's CEO at the time, filed a lawsuit against Microsoft for copyright infringement, though Apple ended up losing it four years later. The court's decision, which allowed Microsoft to sell Windows indefinitely, solidified their place as Apple's largest rival for decades to come. However, the lawsuit was not a total loss for Apple because it did bring a massive amount of publicity and public attention to both companies. But it definitely hurt.

It was Bill Gates, however, who ended up gaining the most personally from the court's decision. The enormous market success of Microsoft Windows led to Bill's net worth rising to over $100 million by 1995, which, according to *Forbes Magazine*, made him the richest person in the world, a distinction he would maintain for decades.

From my perspective, it seemed as though Steve and Bill had always been rivals. Both were incredibly competitive and shared a love for technology, but other than that they did not have a lot in common. Steve was the quintessential left-brain, passionate, creative type, whereas Bill was a programmer and clearly had a more right-brain, methodical mentality. They both wanted to be recognized as inventors, but Steve saw Bill more as a shrewd businessman driven by wealth and power, rather than someone like himself who relied on creativity and innovation in order to change the world. At one Wednesday morning staff meeting I remember Steve saying, "Bill wants to go down in history as Thomas Edison, but unfortunately he will go down as John D. Rockefeller." For the most part his prediction came true.

IMPACT

Years later, toward the middle of the Apple versus Microsoft lawsuit and after I had left Apple, I received an unexpected phone call from Bill. He remembered me having shown him Lisa in the Sneak Preview room and also knew that I had managed Lisa's development. He asked if I would be willing to fly up to Microsoft headquarters and spend the day with him. I knew he wanted to discuss the lawsuit and, even though I had already left Apple (the first time), I still felt a sense of loyalty to Steve, but was still curious to talk to Bill.

I considered whether or not I should go and ultimately took him up on the offer for two reasons. First, I knew I wasn't going to say something that would jeopardize Apple's lawsuit. If anything, I would be able to gain information from Bill and Microsoft's defense of it. Second, he agreed to let me bring along my son, Kris, and I knew visiting Microsoft headquarters and meeting Bill Gates would be a big deal for him. After all, Kris had been a digital native since he was very young, and Bill was one of the most respected engineers and businessmen in the world.

The following week Kris and I flew to Bellevue, Washington, where Microsoft headquarters was located. After getting off the plane I expected to find an intern or assistant waiting to pick us up. Instead, Bill himself picked us up in his Lexus. "Hey, John!" he said with a smile, as if we had been close friends for years. He slid a pile of books and textbooks out of the way in his back seat so that Kris could sit down. Microsoft had just gone public a few years earlier, skyrocketing Bill's net worth. It was unusual that such a high-profile CEO, and one of the richest men in the world, would pick us up from the airport himself. I felt honored and Kris just loved it.

After a short drive, Bill, Kris, and I walked through the buildings on Microsoft's beautiful campus. Bill hadn't said anything about the lawsuit. He did spend quite a bit of time though talking to Kris, who could barely contain his excitement. Once we entered Bill's office he sat behind his desk, looked at Kris and smiled. "Kris, you'll never know the impact your dad had on Microsoft and the computer industry. I thought my company was dead when your dad showed me Lisa. When I got back to Microsoft, I reorganized the whole company." That was an understatement. But it was also a touching moment that I'll never forget, not just because Bill had seen me as having such an influence in the industry, but also because Kris was looking up at me with a huge smile, as if he was the proudest son in the world.

It turned out that what Bill had wanted to talk to me about was an old research project that he had heard of and wanted to learn more about. He said he believed it was at the Zurich Institute of Technology, where I had gone to visit Dr. Niklaus Wirth, the founder of Pascal. The project, Bill explained, was supposedly another graphical user interface that had existed before the Xerox Alto. He was trying to find out if I knew about it, presumably so he could use it as a defense in the Apple lawsuit by contending there was already a workable GUI prior to Lisa. But the truth is I had never even heard of it. So, while Kris and I certainly enjoyed our time hanging out with Bill Gates at Microsoft, I really wasn't of much use to him.

CHAPTER 7

LISA'S LEGACY

"Let's make a dent in the universe."

—STEVE JOBS

From the time I showed Lisa to Bill Gates in Apple's Sneak Preview room, it ended up taking him and Microsoft three full years to emulate the technology, the equivalent amount of time it took us to design and develop it in the first place. I found that puzzling considering all they had to do was reverse engineer and tweak the work we had previously done, while we had to find a way to do things that no one had ever done. No one had ever written and designed code for a commercial graphical user interface other than Xerox PARC, much less for its corresponding applications. But despite the steep learning curve, internal and external competition, dwindling resources and numerous challenges along the way, we eventually pulled it off. On January 19, 1983, after initially being introduced at Apple's shareholders meeting, Lisa was finally introduced to the world during a Boston Computer Society meeting in the New England Life Center.

I had high hopes that everyone would appreciate how innovative and revolutionary Lisa was and that their appreciation would lead to significant sales. I had never been as excited about a product release as I was with Lisa, but I was also worried because I knew we still faced possible consequences related to our pre-release challenges (i.e., Twiggy drives, price points, etc.) Nonetheless, I intended to make the most of the situation and while I had no way of knowing just how much Lisa would go on to influence the future of computers, I was fully aware that I was in the midst of a historical moment in computer history.

After our introductory presentation in Boston, I flew to New York to meet up with Steve for a series of press briefings that took place in a suite at the Carlyle Hotel. A Lisa was set up near a baby grand piano on top of which sat a large bowl of strawberries. I find it amazing how I can always remember minor details from major events. It's confirmation that Steve was right when he frequently told us that tiny details mattered. Make no mistake, the press meeting that day at the Carlyle was a *big* event. This was way beyond just "buzz," closer to what you might call public euphoria. It seemed like none of us could stop smiling. The press snapped hundreds of pictures and asked rapid-fire questions, thrilled that they no longer had to rely on leaks to see the future of personal computers.

From the moment Lisa was introduced right up through the time it shipped, virtually everything in the press about it was positive, with some even hailing it as the "start of a revolution" in computers—the exact thing Steve had hired me to do just five years earlier. Now, here we were reading about our achievement in some of the largest publications in the world, including *The New York Times*, *Time* magazine, *Newsweek*, and all of the relevant trade magazines. Some of the more memorable headlines included:

- "A Hugh Tech Bombshell"
- "It Really Did Blow Our Minds"
- "A Remarkably Friendly Personal Computer"
- "A New Generation of Easy Computing"
- "A Machine that Changes How Computers and People Relate"
- "I Love Lisa"

I have to give Apple credit—they provided an outstanding marketing and publicity campaign around Lisa. I fondly remember our first TV commercial, which featured a young Kevin Costner with the dog, Jumbo Red, from the hit movie *Flashdance*. It began by showing a relaxed Costner riding a bicycle at the break of dawn while his dog walks along beside him. As he continues to spend quality time with his dog, he's clearly in no hurry to get anywhere or do anything. When he finally gets to his office, he sits at his desk, turns on a Lisa on his desk, and begins to work on a graphical user interface by pointing and clicking with a connected mouse. Throughout the commercial the overlapping narration says:

> "The way some businesspeople spend their time has very little to do with a clock. At Apple we understand that business as usual, isn't anymore. That's why we make the most advanced personal computers in the world. And why soon there will be just two kinds of people. Those who use computers. And those who use Apples."

As the commercial nears its end, Costner's telephone rings. He answers it, smiles, and tells the person on the other end (presumably his wife), "Yeah, I'll be home for breakfast." I thought the commercial nicely captured how simple the GUI-based Lisa was to use and its ability for busy people to save time.

There was a print campaign as well that I was fond of that played off of Steve referring to computers as "bicycles for the mind," only this time the ads referred to Lisa as being the "Maserati for the mind." It was also pretty cool to see that some of the articles were describing me as being the "Father of Lisa." While it was flattering, I was only one member of an extremely talented team of designers, coders, developers, marketers, and others that all worked together to bring Lisa to life. I may have been the one fortunate enough to have led that team, but the truth was that Lisa had many fathers.

Nonetheless, one of the perks of my being referred to as the "Father of Lisa" was that I had the opportunity to meet influential people at various high-profile parties and benefits. One of my most memorable was attending *Newsweek*'s 50th anniversary gala and sitting next to Katherine Graham, the longtime publisher of *The Washington Post*. Another highlight was being invited to attend *Newsweek*'s sponsoring of the 24 Hours of Le Mans' 51st Grand Prix of Endurance, at which I got to hang out with Superman himself, Christopher Reeve! While those first few months of 1983 brought some of the most remarkable moments of my life, none compared to the overall joy I had introducing Lisa to the world.

JOHN SCULLEY

One of the last individuals to view Lisa that day in New York was John Sculley who was, at the time, the highly respected president of Pepsi-Cola. Our meeting with him was part of the full court press that Steve had been orchestrating to woo him into leaving Pepsi and becoming CEO of Apple. Me, Steve, and Floyd Kvamme (Apple's head of Marketing and Sales) met with John over dinner that night in New York and talked for hours about Pepsi and Apple. John was universally recognized as the marketing genius behind the "Pepsi Generation" ad campaign. The most successful part of that campaign was the "Pepsi Challenge," in which Pepsi representatives organized blind taste tests that put Pepsi side-by-side against Coke, its primary competitor, in malls and grocery stores across the country. As shoppers passed by their booths the Pepsi team would ask them to stop and try out two different sodas in unmarked cups, one containing Pepsi and the other Coke. Once the shopper tried both, they would be asked which soda they preferred and more often than not they chose Pepsi. When the company started broadcasting the challenge on television it became a huge success and put Pepsi on a more equal level with Coke, which had dominated the market for years.

As John described for us the details of the campaign, we started to wonder if Apple could do something similar. Like Pepsi, we felt that Apple was also trying to target a new generation of computer users. Steve loved the "try before you buy" concept that was at the core of the Pepsi campaign and would eventually do something similar with a "Test Drive Your Mac" campaign in which potential Macintosh users could "borrow" a Mac and test drive it at home for a short period of time. It was essentially a computer lending program, which had never been done before and went a long way toward convincing people that using a personal computer wasn't as difficult as they may have thought.

That same night in New York, I took some time to walk John through the details of "Lisa Technology" and he was blown away. He told us later that he was equally impressed by our passion for Lisa and our ambitious plans to change the world. The four of us remained in that restaurant until it closed, enthusiastically sharing stories, ideas, and visions for the future. And when we finally left we agreed to meet him again for breakfast the next morning! After Steve and I returned to our hotel we were both so pumped about everything that had happened that day that we stayed up all night brainstorming new ideas. Without a wink of sleep and running off pure adrenaline, we met John for breakfast, continuing right where we left off the night before.

After those initial meetings in New York, Steve continued to try and persuade John to join us at Apple. He visited Apple headquarters several times and was clearly considering the idea. It was during one of these visits that Steve asked him the now famous question, "Do you want to continue selling sugar water the rest of your life or do you want to change the world?" That was *definitely* the Steve I knew. The same one who, on my very first time meeting with him, was so inspiring and passionate that he had me on the edge of my seat, ready to help him make history. In his world resistance was futile. If he wanted something (or someone) bad enough, he seemed to always find a way to get it (or them), and this time was no different. On April 8, 1983, John Sculley resigned as president of Pepsi-Cola to become Apple's third CEO.

WAS LISA A FAILURE?

Prior to Lisa shipping, expectations at Apple were high. We knew we had a revolutionary product that no one had ever seen, and we were proud to have set the direction for the future of personal computing. Now we just needed to get Lisa into the hands of as many people as possible and we knew that once they got a taste of the future there would be no going back. After all, going back would be like having an old flip phone from the 1990s, upgrading to the latest iPhone for a few weeks, and then trying to go back to that old phone. That's what we wanted for people who tried Lisa. Once they got a taste of a graphical user interface, we knew there was no way they were going back to text-based operating systems.

Lisa began shipping in June of 1983. Our short-term sales goal was to sell 10,000 Lisas during the second half of the year, even with the limitations of a fifty-person sales team! Despite the extreme $10,000 price tag and unreliable Twiggy drives, we ended up having strong sales to universities and overseas, and we ended up selling over 13,000 units, easily surpassing early expectations. A big reason we had so many sales was because there was nothing else like it in the world. Lisa could do things no other computer could do, and it put other computers to shame. But those early challenges we had faced during development were just not going away.

Remember the ship that leaks from the top? Now that the world was witnessing the power of a graphical user interface and mouse, it was clear that they wanted more. But at $10,000 Lisa was unaffordable to most companies who would normally buy in bulk. This significantly increased the demand for a more affordable GUI-based computer and suddenly the Apple rumor floodgates had reopened. Seemingly everyone began to talk about this new Apple computer they were hearing about (from Steve) that was basically Lisa, but for a lot less money. Thousands of potential customers who had heard about this new computer decided to wait. But they didn't need to wait long because in January of 1984, just seven months after Lisa began shipping, Apple introduced the Macintosh.

As promised, the Macintosh displayed a graphical user interface and a mouse just as Lisa had, but there was one major difference—it only cost $2,500. For the price of one Lisa users could now buy *four* Macintoshes. For nearly anyone wanting a GUI-based computer this was the deal of a lifetime. Although Macintosh was marketed toward individual consumers rather than businesses, as Lisa was, many companies just couldn't resist the massive price difference and purchased them in bulk. Macintosh began to instantly sell units at a record-breaking pace, but things weren't going so well for its big sister, Lisa.

Throughout 1984 Lisa sold around 40,000 units. Those numbers would drop even more in the first half of 1985, which then led to Lisa's discontinuation. But throughout Lisa's two-year life span, around 4,500 units had been sold per month on average, which was very close to Apple's initial sales projections. NASA ended up becoming Lisa's largest customer, purchasing thousands of units at a time, and we ended up selling as many Lisas internationally as we did domestically. In the end the Lisa had sold just over 100,000 units at $10,000 each. That meant that over the course of Lisa's two-year life span, it delivered to Apple $1 billion in revenue (equal to $2.6 billion in 2020 dollars) while costing $50 million to develop.

When people look back on Apple's history there is often a misconception about Lisa being an Apple "failure." But was it? To answer this, let's first look at early sales of Lisa compared to its predecessor, the Apple II. The most similar thing between them was that, at the time of their respective releases, they were both revolutionary. The Apple II was first launched in June of 1977 and went on to sell 100,000 units by the end of 1980, two and half years later. The initial cost of the Apple II was only $1,300, making it a somewhat affordable personal computer. By contrast, it took a $10,000 Lisa just two years to reach the 100,000 sales mark. I'm certainly not implying that Lisa was any better than the Apple II, because they were completely different computers built for different markets and users. But I do find it interesting to compare the two in terms of cost and units sold.

LISA vs MACINTOSH

Comparing Lisa's early sales results to the Macintosh's obviously tells a different story, but even here there are a couple of points to note. As mentioned, the four-year development costs of Lisa Technology were around $50 million, while Macintosh was developed for much less. It cost us so much with

Lisa because we had to pay for research *and* the development of a completely redesigned GUI, mouse, software, and a host of other features. This ended up significantly reducing the development costs for the Mac because we were able to skip much of the research part and leverage Lisa's design and software, which saved Apple time and money.

Macintosh's early sales numbers were extraordinarily high (around 70,000 units in its first three months) compared to Lisa's, but it also sold for a quarter of the price. Macintosh was also released with a full set of Microsoft applications, while Lisa had to be released with just its Office Suite. The Mac was able to benefit from third-party applications very early on but its software could not run on a Lisa. This forced most potential buyers to have to choose between an expensive Lisa or an inexpensive Macintosh.

A year after Lisa began shipping, Apple decided to repackage it as the Lisa 2, sell it for half the price, and give original Lisa owners free hardware upgrades. But doing so left the company without a high-end computer, so they ended up repackaging Lisa a second time just one year later. Rather than calling the new version Lisa 3, Apple finally realized that having two different lines of computers competing against each other made no sense. Coming full circle, Lisa was once again positioned as Apple's high-end computer. In an effort to merge the two product lines its name was changed to "Macintosh XL" and it was given a bigger screen, more memory, and a hard disk. This latest version of Lisa finally included a Migration Kit that consisted of a program called MacWorks, allowing it to run most types of Macintosh software, a feature I had been fighting for since 1980. These changes essentially turned Lisa into a bigger, more powerful and more expensive Macintosh. By 1986, a year after Steve left Apple, the entire line of Lisa products was permanently discontinued, and Macintosh became the company's sole focus. The remaining Lisa computers were sold to a reseller, Sun Remarketing, and would later end up in a landfill, dead and literally buried.

LISA'S INFLUENCE

Although Lisa ended up becoming obsolete just two years after its launch, its influence on every computer that came after, as well as other industries, continues to live on even today. The first and most obvious influence was on Macintosh. At first glance, the original Lisa and the original Macintosh, despite being introduced a year apart, were similar in many ways. They were both built on Lisa Technology and both featured a GUI interface, a mouse, the ability to cut and paste, and multiple proportional fonts with user selectable sizes. But there were also significant differences between the two computers that really set Lisa apart. For example, on the hardware side, only Lisa came with a hard drive, built-in expansion slots, a large, high resolution display, a numeric keyboard, and support for up to 2mb of memory.

There were also key differences on the software side. For example, Lisa's OS came with a screensaver and the ability to multitask and handle multiple operating systems, none of which were available options on Macintosh at the time. There were also five applications on Lisa that were written in Pascal, a higher-level language than the assembly code used to create Macintosh applications. Finally, one of the best things about the Lisa was that it came with Protected Memory, a feature that let users shut down their computer and simply walk away, knowing that all of their data would be automatically saved, just as they had left it. For whatever reason, this feature would not be included as part of the Macintosh for decades.

These were just some of the differences that made Lisa's technology more sophisticated and powerful than Macintosh's and why most Apple engineers at the time believed that developing and marketing Lisa, at a lesser price point, would have been a better choice. Steve Wozniak has even proclaimed that, "Apple should have picked Lisa's OS."

Lisa has also significantly influenced a number of technological innovations beyond just Macintosh. It forever changed the way computers were built and used and reshaped the entire industry in its image. A common misconception is that Apple just copied everything from the Xerox Alto, but the reality was that the Alto was a $50,000 research machine without a user-friendly GUI, business software, or file protection. It lacked basic functionality and suffered from a lack of applications. Lisa was beyond even what the guys at Xerox had imagined. What we took from Xerox PARC was a good idea and improved on it, just as Xerox had done back in 1968 after Engelbard's "Mother of all Demos" presentation.

From my very first day at Apple the task Steve had given me was crystal clear—to build a revolutionary computer that would redefine the nature of personal computing. Because of his vision and the hard work of my extraordinary team, I'm proud to say that we successfully completed that task. I do sometimes hear people say that Lisa "didn't catch on," but they're wrong. It caught on in the form of Macintosh, which would later transform the computer industry in ways consumers couldn't imagine—due specifically to Lisa Technology. In fact, every operating system that exists today has been influenced by Lisa, from Mac OS and iOS to Microsoft Windows and Android. Whether or not people believe Lisa was financially unsuccessful, there could be no disputing the impact it had historically.

What Lisa Introduced to Mainstream Consumers	
Graphical User Interface (GUI)	Ability to drag and drop
Windows-based interface	Ability to copy, edit, cut and paste
Mouse & Cursor	"Clipboard" system for moving data
Virtual "Desktop"	Ability to save & recall documents
Computer "Icons"	Low Power Mode (led to Sleep Mode)
Menu bar	Software/hardware integration
Dropdown menus	Pop up dialogue and alert boxes
Window scroll bars	Easy system disassembly
Zooming Windows to Open/Close	Non-physical file names
Computer "Files and Folders"	Multi-language keyboards
Desktop file manager (led to Finder)	Self-diagnostic startup tests
Protected-memory OS	Screen contrast & dimming
Document-oriented workflow	Task-oriented workflow
Anti-piracy & copy protection	MacWorks migration (led to Bootcamp)
Office Software Suites (i.e. MS Office)	Document password protection
Overlapping windows	Multiple user-selected proportional spaced font
Duplicate file names	Macintosh OS
iOS	Microsoft Windows OS

CHAPTER 8

OUTSIDE, LOOKING IN

"Life goes on and you learn from it."

—STEVE JOBS

By mid-1983 it was clear that Apple's attention would remain on Macintosh as Steve felt strongly that consumer-based products would have a greater market and thus drive Apple's future. I was thankful for having had the opportunity to introduce Lisa to the world but was also a bit disappointed watching the Mac command *all* of Apple's available resources. It was especially difficult watching my talented Lisa team be forced to the outside, looking in, and not receive the recognition they deserved. These frustrations were certainly contributing factors to my forthcoming decision to leave Apple, but the main reason had less to do with work and more to do with home.

TUG-OF-WAR

In the summer of 1983, while vacationing in Japan, I made the decision to resign from Apple. I had been there for the past five years and was fortunate to have worked directly with Steve, who always made me feel like I was a part of something bigger, something that mattered, or as he liked to say, "something *insanely* great." But at the same time, being a part of such a fast-growing startup took a tremendous toll on my family. Fifteen-hour workdays weren't just common at Apple, they were basically required. The Macintosh team was so proud of that they began wearing T-shirts that read, "90 hours a week and loving it!"

Those long hours weren't typically a problem for the hungry, ambitious and single 20-year-olds fresh out of college whom I worked with, but I was now a 36-year-old father of three, with another child on the way, and as Apple continued to rapidly grow, my workload had become increasingly time-consuming. Work at Apple in the early days simply *never* ended. It was all hustle from the time we woke up in the morning to the time we (sometimes) went to sleep late at night. That was the environment I had been used to for years.

But I really began to take a hard look at the situation when I found myself in Japan, supposedly on a combined sabbatical and vacation, but instead just doing press interviews for Apple and writing a software division business plan for John Sculley. After returning to my hotel room, I found a poem written by my seven-year-old daughter, Tiffany, that I felt best expressed the tension between my life at work and at home. It read:

> *I will not play tug of war,*
> *I'd rather play hug of war,*
> *Where everyone hugs instead of tugs,*
> *Where everyone kisses and everyone grins,*
> *And everyone cuddles and everyone wins.*

Her words really hit home and practically had me in tears. I knew that I was the reason this never-ending game of tug-of-war continued, denying my daughter her sought-after hugs, kisses, and cuddles. I was missing out on a large piece of my children's lives and I felt that unless I did something about it nothing would change, even as my wife and I were making plans to bring another child into our lives. The worst part was I knew that if I kept working those long hours at Apple, I would just continue to convince myself that I was doing it *for* my family. The truth was that deep inside I knew that I was financially secure enough at that point that "doing it for my family" was a poor excuse. I really did love working, but I could no longer justify the insane hours. Having lost my own father at five years old, one of my biggest fears was that my children would have to go through life without theirs.

LEAVING APPLE

The main reason I didn't go directly to Steve about my leaving when I returned from Japan was because I knew he would be able to persuade me to stay. Instead, I drafted a resignation letter and submitted it to our head of HR, Ann Bowers, in which I explained to her my reasons for leaving and how difficult it was to have made that decision. The main reason it was so hard was because I felt like I would be bailing on my Lisa team at a time when they were already feeling abandoned by Steve's total focus on Macintosh.

Ann was hesitant to accept my resignation. Over the past several months, she explained, leadership changes at Apple had driven many executives out and the new CEO, John Sculley, had wanted to slow down the mass exodus. She asked if I would wait until she could talk to Sculley and I reluctantly agreed. A few days later Ann called me back into her office and told me that Sculley had asked me to hold off on resigning and to complete my sabbatical. I had no idea resigning could be so difficult! "Instead of resigning," Ann said, "I can keep your resignation letter in a drawer for a few months." Wanting to leave on good terms, I accepted their offer.

During my time away I considered my post-Apple options and realized that a lot of my wealth was in the form of Apple options and that I would need to have access to some of it in order to make the transition. Corporate executives are not allowed to exercise (buy) or sell stock options on the same day, but since I was resigning and needed quick access to some of the money, I told my broker to sell a portion of my stock options. As instructed, he exercised the options but wasn't able to sell the stock before the market closed. The following morning, Apple had a two-digit price drop in its stock value, which meant that I would be receiving significantly less money for my exercised shares.

Losing so much money literally overnight was bad enough, but then it occurred to me that I had exercised the options and sold my stock without considering that I was technically still an Apple executive, meaning the transactions I had just made were *illegal*. Worried that I might get into real trouble over the mistake, I explained to Ann Bowers what happened and asked her to accept the previously dated resignation letter I had submitted, which she agreed to do. And with that, it was official—I was no longer an Apple employee.

Never the one to stress over things I have no control over, I came to accept the fact that my stock option blunder had cost me money, but I was also relieved that my carelessness didn't get me in trouble. I was just glad the whole episode was now behind me, or so I thought.

Not long after my resignation, Apple was sued by a group of stockholders for the sudden drop in its stock price and I was one of the people subpoenaed to appear in court. In the middle of my deposition the plaintiffs' attorneys suggested that the price drop was due to Lisa's faulty Twiggy drives and, because of that, it may have been "insider information" that led me to sell my shares when I did. "If I knew Apple's stock would go down because of Lisa's faults," I said, "why would I wait until the stock dropped and sell for less money per share?" The attorneys just looked at each other, realizing their accusation made no logical sense. One of them then looked at me and said, "No more questions." I was now relieved I had lost the $30 per share, because if the stock had gone up rather than down, I may have faced some hefty insider trading fines.

SAYING GOODBYE

Shortly after resigning I came back to Apple to speak with Steve about my reasons for leaving. After all, he was the reason I had joined Apple in the first place. I wanted to make sure he knew how I felt about him and how much it meant to me to have had such an amazing opportunity. But I also explained how important it was at that stage in my life to be there for my family and to spend more time following my faith.

He completely understood and we ended up having a nice conversation. One of the things that most impressed me about him was how much he had matured over the years in terms of compassion and having more tolerance for those with different beliefs. For example, he had never been a religious person to my knowledge. Once, in the early days at Apple, he had run across a picture of Jesus that one of my interns had hung on her cubicle wall and ripped it down right in front of her. I was shocked, as it was one of the rudest things I had ever seen him do.

But by now he had changed a lot. I was especially impressed by how open-minded he was when I talked about how important it was for me to put more time into my faith. After I was done talking about it, he sat quietly for a moment, looked up at me and said, "John, I understand. While I don't share your conviction, I respect you for having it." That meant a lot.

As I got up to leave, seemingly out of nowhere, Steve said, "You know, you're going to end up in the education field." I have no idea how he came to that conclusion as we had never discussed any such thing. "You think so?" I asked. "When you do," he continued, "take what you've learned here and apply it in ways that will make a difference." I was genuinely confused about his education prophecy, but no matter where I ultimately ended up, I knew his advice was sound. He then glanced slowly up at me from behind his desk and said, "And when you *return*, bring back all the things you've learned."

Even today I have no idea why Steve said that back then, but he was right, because that was exactly what would end up happening. I *did* end up working in education and *would* later apply the lessons I learned during that time upon my return to Apple as, of all things, Vice President of *Education*—an all-new position that he would create for me. He didn't predict the future, he *invented* it!

I was glad that Steve kept in touch after I left and even reached out to me a few times after leaving Apple himself. One of the most memorable moments I had with him during this period was when he invited me to his 30th birthday party, at which everyone there was treated to an unforgettable performance by legendary jazz singer Ella Fitzgerald. Knowing Steve's admiration for Walt Disney, my gift to him that year was a giant Walt Disney book on animation and creativity. It turned out to be an ironic choice because later, he would sell his Pixar animation studio, instantly making him Disney's largest shareholder.

MOVING ON

Despite Steve's apparent prescient ability, I had no idea what I was going to do after leaving Apple, but it didn't take long before interesting opportunities began to arise. The first came by way of an angel investment group that Tom Whitney and I had put together. I ended up investing $250,000 in a company called Lightyear and, for a brief time, helped lead the company as its CEO. Lightyear's product was an "advanced spreadsheet" that would allow users to deal with qualitative data, data that couldn't be defined by a number. It was an interesting idea that we received a lot of press on, even making the cover of making the cover of *PC Magazine*. The problem was that the software only ran on a PC and could not be run on Apple computers, which didn't exactly improve my relationship with Steve. In the end, Lightyear turned out to be a false start and didn't make it, but as my first attempt at a CEO role I learned a lot from the experience, but mostly how to be more careful with my investments and time!

After Lightyear I found myself once again unsure of my next move. One of the good things that came from this period was that I was starting to gain a reputation as an angel investor with executive experience, which was an important combination that brought me opportunities that had never before existed. But by this point I felt I needed a break from the never-ending lure of the Silicon Valley startup scene and began looking elsewhere. Where that was, I did not know, but I *did* know that I needed to focus on one of the main reasons I had left Apple in the first place—to spend more time with family. Back then my wife and I had owned a beach house in Del Mar where she and our kids would go each summer while I remained in the valley buried in work. I didn't get to see them very much during those times, which I regretted. *From this point forward*, I told myself, *I am going to play a much more active role in their lives.*

I ended up selling our Los Gatos home in Northern California and moving with my family to Rancho Santa Fe, a suburb on the north side of San Diego. It felt amazing to be fully committed to my family and faith and having the time to regularly attend church. One of the most important things I had prayed for at the time was direction. God was apparently listening, because at some point I received the parable of the Good Samaritan, telling me to stop worrying about the past and the future and instead find a way to meet a *present* need. It was this direction that helped me identify that one present need had to do with the ongoing struggles of the small school my kids attended, Santa Fe Christian.

SANTA FE CHRISTIAN

Once settled into Southern California, I enrolled my two older children at a small, K-12 private school called Santa Fe Christian Academy (SFC). One day, after dropping my kids off at school, I was approached by a parent who asked me if I would like to join him on the board. I always felt strongly that it was my responsibility as a parent to support my children's education in every way possible. Seeing as how this opportunity also fit in with my calling to meet a present need, I took him up on the offer.

This wasn't my first time being involved in the education field. I had spent time as an acting instructor at UC Berkeley, taught two courses at Cal State San Jose, introduced Apple IIs to St. Mary's school in Los Gatos, which inspired the Apple's Kids Can't Wait program. All of these experiences had created a special place in my heart for education, but I never had time to dig much deeper. Even so, I initially saw my role at Santa Fe Christian as being temporary but ended up falling in love with the students and faculty and decided to stay longer than I had initially planned.

I started my board work at SFC by writing a five-year business plan with two five-year extensions, but in the process, I learned just how bad things were at the school. It was deeply in debt to the tune of $300,000, losing $30,000 a month, and only had a thirty-day lease on the property. My first reaction was, "Oh no, have I made another mistake? I've got to get out of here, because I don't want to mess this up." I felt that I had already failed to save Lightyear and did not want to fail again, especially at something so central to my children's lives. Nonetheless, I needed to adhere to my commitment. I felt the Lord ask, "I have blessed your entire life with a family, the opportunity at Apple, and financial resources, and now the first time that you can't see the light at the end of the tunnel, you're going to run?" It was such a powerful message that I decided to turn the results over to the Lord and committed 100 percent to reviving the school.

As I was preparing to write that initial SFC business plan, the first thing that stood out was the lack of vision for the school. One of the key takeaways from working with Steve was that he always had a clear vision for Apple and knew exactly *why* we were in business. "If you don't know why your school exists or where you want to go," I told the board bluntly, "the one thing I can guarantee you is that you'll never get there." The business plan I wrote was based on a demographic study I conducted around a ten-mile radius of the school. It showed that 60 percent of the people who lived near the school had some form of higher education, yet SFC had no AP or honor courses and none of our graduates had ever attended an Ivy League college. I even learned through interviews that many parents would drive right past our school, traveling ten or more miles to schools that did focus on college prep. It was clear that the number one problem at SFC was that the school wasn't meeting the needs of its community.

THE CALLING

While I could have proposed making Santa Fe a college-prep school by adding an admissions filter and only accepting kids with high test scores and great short-term memories, for me that was never really an option. My faith was strong, and I believed that I had a mission directly from a higher power who was saying, "I want you to build a school for all of my children, not just the wealthy ones." This specific calling would not allow me to turn my back on kids who needed help—a calling that would stay with me for the rest of my life.

I continued supporting SFC for the next ten years, including helping them purchase the ten acres of land the school sat on and getting them completely out of debt. I still recall a vivid dream I had around this time in which I was on a boat throwing life preservers to people who were drowning and hearing the warning, "At some point, a day will come when people will argue about the color of their life preservers." After reflecting on this, I knew that at some point SFC leadership would begin taking things for granted, and that would be the day I would need to move on, free from God's calling there, and find another present need.

Once we got the school out of debt and successfully purchased the land, things were finally looking up, but one thing I knew we still needed to do was build a gymnasium for our students. During a board meeting I made an enthusiastic pitch about the importance of having a gym and argued that we should begin designing and building one right away. But the head of the finance committee disagreed, insisting that we raise all of the funds for it before even beginning the process. I promised them the money would come, but there was again disagreement and I was overruled. It was then that I realized they were now arguing over the color of life preservers and I tendered my resignation for the end of the academic year.

I had been hosting a Christmas party at my home every winter for SFC board members and rather than break that tradition I decided to host one more before leaving. During the party I was approached by one of the finance committee members who had been against my gym idea. "I've been thinking a lot about what you said, and you were right," she admitted. "We've left no room in our numbers for the Lord to work." As it turned out the committee had changed their minds and began building the gym prior to securing all of the funding, just as I suggested. It was fully paid for within months.

BIG CHANGES AT APPLE

While at Santa Fe Christian I continued keeping a close eye on the many changes happening at Apple, some of which I didn't think were good. One that stood out to me was Steve Wozniak's growing level of concern over the lack of investment in the Apple II program. Back in 1981, Woz's plane accident had put him out of commission for an extended period of time. After his return he was still disappointed to see that Apple had continued to shift resources away from his Apple II (still the best-selling personal computer in the world), and toward the significantly flawed Apple III. Now, years later, Apple was once again turning its back on the Apple II, this time for the Macintosh, despite the fact that the Apple II had accounted for nearly 85 percent of Apple's sales, even with Macintosh in the market.

But Woz's frustrations this time weren't so much about Apple's focus on Macintosh as they were about his feeling that his Apple II team wasn't getting the credit and the respect they deserved, not unlike the feelings I had about my Lisa team. Even so, a fight with Apple's current leadership was one that Woz knew he would lose. So, he instead shifted his attention to a new invention, a single-button remote-control that he and a colleague had designed. Not surprisingly, Apple showed zero interest in the device, which then drove Woz to tender his resignation and leave Apple to further pursue new endeavors.

Meanwhile, things weren't going so well for Steve Jobs either, as he and then-CEO John Sculley were finding themselves more frequently at odds, something that came as a bit of a surprise to many people. I couldn't help but remember how close Steve and Sculley had once been. Ever since Steve and I had hung out with him that night in New York City, the two had become virtually inseparable. As late as November of 1984 they were perceived as being on the same page, so much so that an issue of *BusinessWeek* magazine featured them on the cover under the headline "Apple's Dynamic Duo: And Their Bold Plan to Take on IBM in the Office." But now things between them had clearly changed. Things came to a boiling point when Steve started publicly disagreeing with Sculley, making him feel as though his authority was constantly being undercut.

One key issue that divided them came about as Macintosh continued to struggle to gain traction in the consumer market. Sculley had agreed with Woz's sentiment that Apple needed to commit more resources toward their big moneymaker, the Apple II, rather than focusing exclusively on Macintosh, but Steve vehemently disagreed. He had gone all-in on Macintosh for years and refused to even entertain the idea of Apple shifting any of its focus toward another computer. Steve had no longer viewed Sculley as Apple's savior. Their growing public disagreements ultimately led to Steve's failed coup and subsequent resignation. He was so frustrated by the situation that he promptly sold all of his Apple stock, with the exception of a single share. That would have been a pretty big deal to most people because at the time of his departure he owned around 11 percent of Apple, which was worth around $130 million at the time, equivalent to around $66 billion today. But for Steve it didn't matter because to him standing on principle was worth a lot more.

It had been less than a year since *BusinessWeek's* "Dynamic Duo" article, and already major newspapers and magazines began to tell a different story. *Fortune's* August 1985 cover read: "The Fall of Steve Jobs" and a month later *Newsweek's* September 1985 cover took it even further saying: "A Whiz Kid's Fall: How Apple Computer Dumped Its Chairman." The media was now framing Steve's departure as being a significant fall from grace.

As I watched all of this, from the outside, looking in, I was disappointed that Apple had essentially forced out a true creative genius, much less a founder who built the company from scratch. In my opinion it was Apple that was making the bigger mistake as they had an opportunity to continue profiting off of Steve's incredible vision and chose not to. They now found themselves without either of its founders and would soon begin a twelve-year downturn that would take the company to the brink of disaster. Meanwhile, Steve started a new computer company, NeXt, allowing him to regain full control over major decisions and freeing him to build, design, and market his computers however he chose.

CHAPTER 9

OPPORTUNITY KNOCKS

*"I've always been attracted to the more
revolutionary changes."*

—STEVE JOBS

Ten years after joining the board at Santa Fe Christian Academy, I again found myself at a crossroads in life and unsure of my future. Now that my children were grown, I found that I had nearly unlimited options on where to live and what to do. Retirement wasn't really an option, because I had given a lot of money away and had been without a salary for ten years. I have also been someone who loves to work. For me, sitting around doing nothing isn't a dream come true, but a waste of time, more akin to a nightmare.

After I left Apple I was asked to return twice by Mike Markkula. The first time I met with the Education Sales VP, who seemed to care more about his compensation package than taking the types of bold risks that had built Apple, which was a big turnoff and I politely passed. The second meeting I took was with new CEO Gil Amelio, and it didn't take me long to realize that I didn't want to work for him either. He clearly wasn't a good fit at Apple and never could understand the company's unique culture. Luckily, everyone realized this quickly and he only lasted a year and a half. Ironically, it was Gil's cultural ignorance that eventually led to Steve returning to Apple, so he did accomplish *one* good thing while he was there! Both of those meetings helped confirm that the time was just not right for me to return. Apple had changed and wasn't the same place I knew and loved. But I never wrote off the idea of eventually returning.

I began brainstorming possible opportunities for my future and ultimately, after realizing how much I missed the entrepreneurial challenges, decided to move back to Silicon Valley and focus on investing. One of my earlier investments had been with the Mayfield Fund, a prominent venture capital firm that focused on early-stage to growth-stage investments and had funded some of the biggest names in tech including 3COM, Amgen, SanDisk, and Compaq. Over time I had grown closer with Mayfield's leadership team and would even go on to become an adviser. In 1997 I joined Mayfield as an "Executive in Residence," meaning I was an in-house consultant who they would loan out to their investment startups. It was my job to help these startups create strategic business plans and to bring in strong leadership that could help founders realize their visions. I was typically assigned to several companies at once but was later asked to focus entirely on one key investment.

AN OFFER YOU CAN'T REFUSE

Pangea Systems was founded by two promising entrepreneurs in Oakland, California in 1991 and sold "enterprise software solutions" to drug companies, biotech companies and academic research. Their focus was bioinformatics, which at the time I could barely spell, much less understand. Bioinformatics is a scientific field in which software tools and methods utilize computational biology to understand large and complex biological data. Specifically, in Pangea's case, the data was related to genomics and its business model was to provide software that researchers can use to search genetic databases.

I knew little about Pangea's co-founders except that they were engineers, scientists, and recent Stanford graduates. They were unusual individuals, somewhere between eccentric and genius, who would eventually go on to create a technology that generated smell! But when I first met them, they just wanted to grow Pangea into a bioinformatics powerhouse that would rival their two largest competitors, Incyte Pharmaceuticals and Celera Genomics. The biggest challenge for Pangea at the time was that they were in the business of writing *custom* software, and anything that's custom made is nearly impossible to scale. I explained this fundamental problem to them and offered up a couple of ideas. After the meeting, I learned that the co-founders had liked my ideas and asked if I'd consider becoming the company's CEO. I just laughed it off because I was the epitome of an outsider who knew next to nothing about their indus-try. Even if the offer was serious, I fully expected the bosses at Mayfield to reject the idea outright, but I was in for a surprise.

That Friday afternoon, at four o'clock, I was summoned into a board meeting. In attendance were Pangea's co-founders, and executives from Pangea's major investors, which included Mayfield, and Kleiner-Perkins, one of the most successful and respected venture capital firms in the world. "John, we have an opportunity for you," Pangea's CEO said to me just as I took a seat. "How would you like to be CEO of Pangea?" Every-one around the table quietly looked at me, smiling, anxiously awaiting an answer. Suddenly, the crazy idea I had laughed off just days earlier wasn't so funny. I hadn't even had time to pro-cess the suggestion, but they clearly were expecting an answer right there on the spot.

To be clear, I was definitely excited about the opportunity to learn a new field and become CEO of a promising startup, especially considering I had been out of the game for so long. But I was reluctant to take on that kind of position in an in-dustry I knew nothing about; not to mention Pangea's offices were over fifty miles away from where I lived, meaning I would have to commute both ways during rush hour when California freeways were parking lots. Both of these factors were big turnoffs for me and I was leaning toward declining the offer. But succeeding in Silicon Valley is based heavily on relationships and disappointing the wrong people often comes with consequences. It would have been risky for me to say no to such an influential and powerful group of people who had already invested a lot in Pangea and were basically asking me for a favor. "Sure," I said, flashing a forced smile. "That'd be amazing."

Later that night I was kicking myself for committing to such a major undertaking without even so much as asking for a day or two to think it over. But it was too late for that, so I knew I had to find a way to make it work. I stayed up nearly all night researching the bioinformatics industry, eventually dozing off at my desk at dawn. But a few hours later my phone rang and jolted me awake. It was eight o'clock on a Saturday morning and I could barely hold my head up straight because I was so tired. But calls at odd hours on weekends are often bad news, so I quickly answered: "Hello?" A jubilant and familiar voice replied, "Hey John, it's Steve Jobs!" I was surprised to hear from him because it had been a while since we last spoke. He wasted no time in getting to the point. "I'm going back to Apple," he said. "I want you to come with me."

Unbelievable! I thought to myself. Sixteen hours after accepting the Pangea job, Steve was now asking me to join him in what I knew would be the rebirth of the Apple I loved. I wanted to say yes and join him, but I had already made a commitment, promising Pangea's founders and investors that I would do what I could to help.

I explained the situation to Steve and reluctantly turned down his offer. He was disappointed but respected the commitment to keeping my word and wished me well. "Call me when you're free," he said. "You'll always be welcome back." Ironically, the following week, when the Pangea co-founders learned that Steve had tried to recruit me back to Apple, they upped my stock options, fearing that I might change my mind.

PANGEA SYSTEMS

I became Pangea's CEO in early 1997. By the time I started I had discovered the tremendous potential of bioinformatics to transform the life science industry and I was actually excited to get started. What I lacked in knowledge of computational biology, I hoped to make up with management experience, by defining a clear vision and inspiring others to work together toward realizing it. This was one of the key skills I learned from Steve while I was at Apple. In fact, there were a lot of skills, lessons, and perspectives that I would bring to Pangea that I learned during the time I spent at both Apple and at Santa Fe Christian.

One of the most important of these was something I learned at Apple and later reinforced at SFC—the understanding that *everyone* is uniquely gifted, and the best leaders are able to motivate others by helping them recognize and take advantage of their individual gifts. It sounds obvious, but too often, even today, groups of people are treated by some managers, teachers, and board members as if they were all the same. But no two people are the same and treating them as such hurts productivity and stymies potential. Every day I spent at Pangea reconfirmed for me, even from a scientific perspective, just how different and unique we all are, from our personalities, talents, and abilities, right down to our DNA. At Apple Steve prided himself at recognizing and developing individual talent among those of us who worked for him and it was exactly what I wanted to do at Pangea.

Other things I brought with me from Apple to Pangea was an attempt to replicate Steve's sheer tenacity, his ability to hyper focus on the things that mattered, his acute sense for marketing flair and especially his visionary leadership. I had even created a leadership model from my experience at Apple called "Leadership by Vision." It provided a detailed roadmap showing leaders how to properly articulate a vision, how to clarify a mission, and how to motivate stakeholders to think creatively. I had used the model as a means to motivate my Lisa team at Apple and it later played a key role in turning around Santa Fe Christian. A summarized version of the Leadership by Vision model looks like this:

- Vision clarifies one's mission
- It provides uniqueness in one's strategic directions
- It promotes creativity of one's tactical steps
- It makes companions, rather than competitors, of the people on the journey
- It frees people to think differently

This was the model I relied on to put Pangea on a path toward the future. During this process we wanted a name that better reflected our vision and we ultimately decided to rename the company DoubleTwist, a play on the double-helix structure of DNA. We also developed a completely unique bioinformatics platform that would be able to better assist scientists and students in their analysis of human genome sequences. Whether they were in academic research or in the biotech community, we wanted to empower anyone doing molecular research in the same way that Apple empowered a new generation of computer users. Changing the world may be exciting, but it's never easy.

One of the most pressing challenges I faced early on in my new leadership role was trying to figure out how to gain access to a supercomputer without having the resources. We needed a supercomputer in order to effectively and efficiently process the data in the human genome, but as a fledgling start-up we didn't have the funds to buy or even rent one. I brain-stormed ways of overcoming this challenge and then I recalled an experience I had with pilot manufacturing at Apple.

I remembered how we used to "burn in" our computers by running software on them for 30 days, and how our hard-ware engineers also used it to test the reliability of hardware components. I wondered if I could now reach out to a hard-ware company that requires powerful software to test their ma-chines and ask them if they would consider using our genome software as a burn-in test. I figured it was worth a try. It would also be a great example of one of my Apple Banners of Innova-tion: "Throw creativity at a problem, not the checkbook."

Ken Okin was an old friend and had been one of my for-mer hardware engineers at Apple. I had heard that he was now working at Sun Computers, a major technology company that tested powerful computers on a daily basis. I gave Ken a call, explained my idea, and asked if he would consider using our software algorithms to test within the burn-in process for their computers. He said they had around 100 Sun supercomputers, that he liked the idea of being part of something on the cutting edge of science and agreed to burn in Sun computers using our software. I was thrilled. He had given us a unique opportunity that provided my team at Pangea a great example of how they could use creativity to solve problems, and also the importance of building, fostering, and leveraging relationships.

Having access to a supercomputer now allowed us to com-pete with bigger competitors, which came as quite a shock to them, as this virtually unknown startup had seemingly come out of nowhere to challenge them. They had all invested mil-lions of dollars to do their own private data sequencing and were successfully selling data to drug companies. But now, here was this new player that was generating their own databases by using *public* data, allowing them to bypass the cost of private sequencing. I kept imagining their CEOs at a conference table, screaming at their execs, "Who ARE these guys???"

DOUBLETWIST

Much of the work we were doing at DoubleTwist involved collaborations with other scientists on the Human Genome Project (HGP), an international scientific research project funded by the U.S. government through the National Institutes of Health. Launched in 1990, that project's goal was to determine the base pairs that make up human DNA, and to identify and map all of the genes of the human genome. It was pretty complex stuff. Somehow, I had now found myself in the same scientific world as Celera's founder, the legendary biochemist and geneticist Craig Venter, as well as industry titans like Randell Scott from Incyte, and Hamilton Smith, an esteemed microbiologist and Nobel Prize laureate.

DoubleTwist was built first and foremost around simplicity. Just as I had done with Lisa at Apple, I added a graphical user interface to the DoubleTwist platform that made it fast, easy, and available to virtually any researcher or scientist. Anyone could now take their genetic profile and freely use our search agents to scour gene libraries and determine their dispositions to diseases that could potentially be treated through gene therapy. We were able to make this possible by aggregating data from multiple sources and then making that data available through software "agents" that acted like mini search engines. A computer would then take a complex query from a user and deploy our software agents to search the internet for specific gene patterns, comparing them to known and unknown sequences. The agents then sent their findings directly to the user.

From the moment I began making sense of genetic profiling, I felt strongly that the work we were doing was as important as it was fascinating. But before I started at DoubleTwist I had no idea what any of this technology was or the role we played in it. Even as I began to get a better feel for it all, I knew we would eventually need to find a way to explain it to reporters, potential investors, and anyone else who didn't happen to be a computational biologist. This was complex science, so if I expected it to become mainstream, I needed to be able to simplify what we did and communicate *why* it was so important.

I began the simplification process by asking people to think of us as the "Yahoo for scientific research." Yahoo was a popular *generalized* search engine (pre-Google) that let people search the web for news, I explained, whereas we were a *specialized* search engine that let scientists search patents, publications, and genetic sequences. But while Yahoo provided a way for users to manually search for things, our search agents did all of the research for them, which was a novel idea at the time. The Yahoo analogy seemed to have worked, and once people had a clearer understanding of what we were doing, we began attracting both investors and media attention. The most prominent media coverage we received at the time came from a *New York Times* article published on September 20, 1999 with the headline, "Surfing the Human Genome; Data Bases of Genetic Code are Moving to the Web." The article went a long way toward introducing us to the world.

THINKING DIFFERENT(LY)

Apple board member Mike Markkula was always telling us that Apple wasn't a personal computer company, but that it was a *lifestyle* company. He was right, because computers (as well as any product or service) don't sell themselves. It was Apple's marketing efforts that brought their computers to life by positioning the brand in a specific way that would appeal to people who were creative and ambitious. There was one campaign in particular that significantly boosted Apple's brand awareness by clearly showcasing exactly who the company was, what it stood for, and who it was targeting. After he returned to Apple, Steve orchestrated one of the most memorable and impactful marketing campaigns in history. Apple's "Think Different" campaign inspired millions of people, including myself. It consisted primarily of posters and TV commercials that featured an array of creative geniuses. Actor Richard Dreyfuss narrated the TV ad, which ended up winning an Emmy Award for Best Commercial as well as the Grand Effie Award for the most effective ad campaign in America. The ad was simple and to the point:

> *"Here's to the crazy ones, the misfits, the rebels, the troublemakers, the round pegs in the square holes... the ones who see things differently— they're not fond of rules... You can quote them, disagree with them, glorify or vilify them, but the only thing you can't do is ignore them because they change things... they push the human race forward, and while some may see them as the crazy ones, we see genius, because the ones who are crazy enough to think that they can change the world, are the ones who do."*

The message of the "Think Different" campaign is what inspired me to create a DoubleTwist culture that encouraged everyone to "think ahead," rather than focusing only on the present. One of the best examples of doing this myself came during my inaugural year as CEO when I traveled east to the genomic industry's most well-known and respected conference, which was hosted by The Institute for Genomic Research (TIGR). Being used to Apple-style events that were large and extravagant, I headed to the convention picturing an enormous conference room packed with breathtaking exhibitions and genius scientists shuffling rapidly from booth to booth. I was wrong.

I first realized that my preconceived notions were wrong the moment I pulled into the parking lot of the hotel, which was not very big considering it was hosting such a major event. I wondered if I was even at the right place and, once inside, I asked one of the hotel staff to confirm it. After assuring me that I was, she escorted me to a small elevator and, to my shock, pushed the "down" button. The only thing down from the first floor was the basement and that's exactly where I was taken.

Now I'm not a snob who needs to be in a luxury hotel, it's just that I *expected* it to be in one because of the hype around it in the scientific community. From my perspective, it was equivalent to Apple announcing a new product event and then hosting it in a trailer! As we stepped out of the elevator, I was once again surprised to find a relatively small crowd of quite normal-looking scientists standing in front of poster board presentations that were more akin to ones found at high school science fairs than professional conferences. I knew right away that if we wanted genomics, and DoubleTwist in particular, to be taken seriously by investors, and the public, a lot more needed to be done. *What's needed*, I thought to myself, *was a bit of good old-fashioned Apple marketing flair!*

MARKETING FLAIR

Startups don't typically have large marketing budgets, if any, but I needed to find a way to at least get the ball rolling.

On my second trip to the TIGR conference I brought boxes full of tchotchkes to hand out. Anyone who came to our booth would get balls that lit up when they were bounced. It wasn't much but it was better than nothing. The following year I hired an Austin Powers look-alike who roamed through the conference uttering phrases in his best British accent such as, "Hey, baby... have you seen DoubleTwist?" The year after that I handed out 10-inch scientist dolls in lab coats and even hired 5'10" dark-haired actors in lab coats who walked around as representations of our software agents. There were two of them in the morning, but then they started to double every two hours, to four, then eight, etc. The genetics guys got a real kick out of that.

One really cool thing that significantly increased our publicity at the 2000 TIGR conference happened on the first day. I wanted to get us more mainstream media coverage and had been inspired by the *New York Times* article that had been written about us a year earlier. This time I took it a step further and had reached out to Andy Pollack, the *New York Times* reporter who had interviewed me at the Carlyle Hotel during Lisa's introduction. This time around I explained, in layman's terms, about the potential world of genomic research and, more specifically, bioinformatics. I described the innovative things we were doing at DoubleTwist and referred back to the previous *Times* article to bolster our credibility. My pitch must have worked, because Andy ended up doing a detailed interview with me that led to a second *New York Times* article, published on May 9, 2000, with the headline, "105,000 Genes Identified in Public Data." But what really made the article work was the way that I leveraged it at the TIGR conference the day it was published.

I was fortunate that the *Times* article was published on the paper's front page on the very first day of the TIGR conference. Once I realized this was going to happen, I bought hundreds of copies of the newspaper and strategically placed them around the TIGR conference floor. This meant that as soon as conferencegoers walked in they could pick up a free copy of the *Times* and see our article splashed across the front page.

While some may see all of these bits of marketing flair as simple gimmicks, they clearly worked because once this second *Times* article reached the paper's 1.2 million subscribers, everyone in the industry, and beyond, began talking about DoubleTwist. We received a lot of new media attention from various sources, greatly expanded our client list, which included major industry names like Merck, Roche, and Hitachi, and ended up raising over $75 million. Things were seemingly going better than ever. After a lot of hard work, I had found myself about to experience my second IPO. Then came the perfect storm.

A PERFECT STORM

In hindsight I realize how fortunate I was to have joined Apple at the perfect time, just as the personal computer revolution was starting and everyone was eager to be a part of it. This time around I was not so lucky. After the May 2000 publication of the *Times* article, and the well-timed TIGR conference, genomics was picking up steam publicly and over the next four months DoubleTwist would become a hot property. Then, on September 11, 2001, the World Trade Center in New York City was attacked by terrorists. The tragic event not only took the public's mind off of everything else in the world, including genomics, but it also shut down the financial markets and any hope of most companies going public. But the WTC attacks were really just one problem. There were other things at play that foretold we were headed for a serious timing challenge.

The trouble really began before my first year was even over. By the fall of 1997 the Asian financial crisis had crashed the global stock market, playing a major role in the start of a recession in the United States. A few years later the "Dot-com bubble" burst, causing thousands of online startups to lose value, or be put out of business altogether, as investors began backing out once they realized the value of the business models were flawed.

While this investor fear was related to online businesses, it ultimately led to a general fear of *all* tech-based startups, which sank their values overnight and put many of them out of business as well. And in case this external perfect storm wasn't bad enough for DoubleTwist, I was personally going through one of the most difficult times in my life. During this same period my wife had decided to file for divorce, which took a major toll on me mentally, emotionally, and physically. This perfect storm swept through my entire four years at DoubleTwist. While I should have been more cognizant of these early warning prior to accepting the job, I could never have predicted such a massive storm. DoubleTwist had taken a direct hit and was eventually sold to Hitachi at a decreased value. In early 2002 I resigned as CEO.

I believe the work we did at DoubleTwist during my tenure was worthwhile and had a positive impact on individuals and on the future of the life sciences industry. Our innovative algorithms and use of technology ended up becoming a precursor to what bioinformatic and mainstream genetic companies, such as 23andMe and Ancestry.com, are doing today. It also helped pave the way for highly sophisticated technologies like CRISPR—clusters of regularly interspaced short palindromic repeats—which is now being used to correct genetic defects and to treat and prevent the spread of diseases.

After leaving DoubleTwist I once again found myself in what was starting to become familiar territory, a state of not knowing the next dot of my life. Then, in March of 2002,

I recalled my previous conversation with Steve, in which he asked me to give him a call when I was free. By this point, he had already begun turning Apple around and laying the groundwork for what would become the greatest second act in modern business history. Just as he had asked me to do, I gave him a call and he was thrilled that I was finally free of my DoubleTwist responsibilities. We caught up a bit and then he said something that was music to my ears. "Ready to come home?" he asked me. While I had turned down all of the earlier opportunities I had to return to Apple, now that Steve was back in charge, I knew the traditional corporate culture the company had descended into was now history. The navy had been washed away and the pirates were back in charge. I had been on the outside, looking in, for long enough.

"I'm ready," I told him. "Great! I have some cleanup to do before I can tell you what role I need you for," he said. "But I'm glad you're coming back." The perfect storm was now in the past and I was headed home, just in time for the future.

CHAPTER 10

BACK FOR THE FUTURE

"We are inventing the future."

—STEVE JOBS

At the end of my phone call with Steve, he asked me to come by and meet the rest of team. When I arrived at Apple headquarters, I was excited, but also a bit nervous for a couple of reasons. First, it had been seventeen years since I left, and I was now entering an Apple that was in many ways unrecognizable. Nearly all of those I had worked with in the past were gone and I was a lot older than most of the Apple's current employees. *Would the younger people at Apple respect my prior experience or view me as someone out of touch with modern technologies?* But the bigger point of anxiety was that Steve hadn't told me what role and challenges I would have this time around. Last time it was clear, I was to "build a revolutionary personal computer." But this time I had no idea what he wanted me to do. This was my first time ever accepting a job offer in which I didn't know the job being offered!

About twenty minutes after I arrived, Steve came out to greet me with a smile and open arms. "Welcome home, John," he said, instantly calming my nerves. "I'm glad to be home," I assured him. "We're changing the world—*again*—and I need to surround myself with people I trust," he told me as we began walking down the hall. "I don't want a bunch of yes-men, I want talented people like yourself who are willing to stand up to me and tell me when I'm wrong," he said. He had said similar things to me before, but it meant a lot to hear him say it again after all these years. We continued our walk down hallways that were bigger than our entire office in 1978. Things had certainly changed a lot, but it was reassuring that at least Steve was still just Steve. "Let me show you around and introduce you to the team," he said.

I ended up going through a day of interviews, at which I met with Apple's VP of Product Marketing, Phil Schiller, Chief Financial Officer, Fred Anderson, Chief Operating Officer, Tim Cook, and a few other high-level executives. Everyone was polite, capable, and clearly shared a single vision for Apple. There was no pressure during the interviews because Steve had already made up his mind that he wanted me back, which made these more meet-and-greets than tests.

At the of the day, I met with Steve in his office and assured him the meetings went fine. "But it's kind of tough when I don't know what the job is you want me to do," I told him. Wearing a look of deep thought, he leaned back in his chair and said, "As a former Apple executive you're a known quantity and I definitely want you here in some capacity, but I haven't decided whether I want you to run applications or education." I was relieved and immediately relaxed now I had at least some idea of what to expect. "I'll make my decision once I clean up a few loose ends," he said. As a seasoned manager and software engineer, I knew I could run the applications group easily enough and after spending a decade at Santa Fe Christian, I would have felt just as comfortable overseeing education. To be honest, I was thrilled to be back no matter what role I would ultimately be given. On April 3, 2002, at the ripe old age of 55, I was once again teaming up with Steve Jobs at Apple.

EDUCATION DIVISION

On my first official day of work I was given two items: my Apple ID, which included my old employee number, and an office next to Phil Schiller. I was also given the opportunity to have a couple of months to experience Apple's new culture, learn its strengths and weaknesses, and get a better understanding of where we were heading. After getting the general lay of the land I began to take a closer look at the two areas that Steve was considering me to lead.

I started by looking at the applications group. I noticed a few things that could have been improved, but for the most part it was in fairly good shape. *If this is the job Steve wants me to do then this will be a breeze*, I thought to myself. *A few changes here and there and this division would practically be running itself.* I really didn't see it as much of a challenge, unless Steve had an entirely new direction for it planned. I then took a look at Apple's education division and came to the conclusion that it was an absolute mess. *Whoever had to fix this was going to need more than just a breeze, they were going to need gale force winds!*

The first thing I learned was that Apple's education business had suffered eight years straight of declining revenue. Knowing how savvy the company's sales and marketing team had become over the years, I wondered how this could have happened. Then I realized that it wasn't much of an education business at all, but more like an afterthought. For starters, the entire "division" was not really a division at all, but two separate groups that were hopelessly divided. Rather than having a single VP of Education who oversaw both sales and marketing, there was a VP of Education Sales *and* a VP of Education Marketing. They were geographically separated and were being led by VPs with different management styles, different agendas, and different visions, neither of which were in line with Steve's overall vision. Each VP also had no idea what the other one was doing, because they didn't care for each other and rarely spoke. To make matters worse, they reported to two different bosses, with marketing reporting to Phil Schiller and sales reporting directly to Tim Cook. It was no wonder Apple was struggling in the education market!

By summer it had become quite clear that, based on leadership issues alone, fixing Education would be much more difficult than managing Applications. During the first week of June, Steve called me to his office and before I could even sit down, he stood up with a smile. "John, I've made up my mind," he said. "I want you to run Apple's education division." Somehow, I knew he was going to say that. "To be honest, I don't know if the problem is a marketing issue or a sales issue," he confessed. I laughed, saying, "Oh, it's definitely both!" He put his hand on my shoulder and said, "Just fix it or I'll have to get us out of the education business." With that, I had now become Apple's first Vice President of Education. The following day Steve sent out the following company-wide email:

> *From: Steve Jobs <sjobs@apple.com>*
> *Subject: New Education Business Unit*
> *Date: June 6, 2002 at 11:43:08 AM CDT*
> *To: apple_employees$@group.apple.com*
> *Reply-To: response@apple.com*
>
> *For over 25 years Apple has led the way in applying technology to education. The education market is part of our DNA. Like most markets, the education market has become very competitive. While we are continuing to innovate with new products, like the eMac, Xserve, Mac OS X and Remote Desktop, we also recognize the need to be more*

*cohesive and responsive with our education
sales and marketing efforts. To better serve the
students, teachers, administrators and parents
that are our customers, we are combining our
education sales and marketing teams to create
a single education business unit that's over 750
people strong.*

*I am pleased to announce that John Couch, a
former VP/GM of Apple, is returning to Apple
to head this unit as our new Vice President,
Education. Both the education sales team, led
by Jim Marshall, and the education marketing
team will report to John. John will report
to Tim Cook. As Apple's original executive
responsible for software, a former headmaster
of a private school, and most recently the CEO
of a life sciences company, John brings many
years of experience in both education and
management to this new role. Please join me
in welcoming John back to Apple.*

—Steve

My primary challenge as Apple's new head of education wasn't just to stop our sales decline, but to significantly grow the business and recover our dominance in the education market. When I left, Apple's education market share was in the 80 percent range and now it was down to single digits. Unfortunately, when an entirely new position is created there's no playbook to follow. You're forced to make it up as you go, without knowing what works and what doesn't—until after you've actually tried it. This was certainly not going to be an easy task, but then again, nothing ever was at Apple. During my first week in this new position, one of my colleagues, Greg Josyiak, who oversaw the iPod program, patted me on the shoulder and declared, "You now have the toughest job in the company, good luck."

FRIENDS OF JIM

One of the most critical areas I needed to deal with right away was figuring out what to do about sales. Shortly after I started looking at our education sales challenges, Steve said to me, "I think you'll end up firing your Sales VP within a year." I doubted that would be necessary, because my Leadership by Vision model was capable of motivating people to join in a shared vision. I only had to fire two people during my earlier years at Apple and none at DoubleTwist, so I was confident that I could work with Jim, our head of sales. I heard that he also had a good relationship with our COO, Tim Cook, who he directly reported to, which gave me even more incentive to make things work.

Jim had been Apple's Vice President of Education Sales for several years, but for whatever reason he chose to base his sales team out of Atlanta, Georgia instead of Cupertino like all other VPs. By the time I started, he had already built a considerable team of people who Cupertinos referred to as "FOJs," short for "Friends of Jim." I assumed people around Apple were over-reacting when they described him to me in ways that made him sound more like a general than a VP. But that was before I actually met the guy.

I flew to Atlanta to meet Jim and his "friends" and to try and figure out why we needed to have an Atlanta-based field office at all. Upon my arrival I saw right away what others meant by their descriptions of Jim as he was quite an intimidating figure. He was a big man who looked and acted like an actor who might be cast as a no-nonsense general in a Hollywood war movie. He was very confident, if not cocky, notorious for running a tight ship, and his employees (aka "friends") were loyal and dedicated to a fault.

On my very first visit I watched as Jim stormed around the office like a four-star general, peering over the shoulder of his FOJ army, barking orders, and micromanaging every detail. But the root of the sales problem wasn't so much his management style, it was that the culture he had created was inconsistent with the one Steve had spent years fostering. I felt more like I was walking through the hallways at IBM rather than Apple. Nearly all of Jim's soldiers appeared to be corporate, ex-IT types and he was blatantly building a sales organization based on IT-services rather than focusing on how Apple's existing products could improve learning. His sales philosophy revolved around focusing on features (technical aspects of products) over benefits (*why* what we're selling matters). It's the classic *what* versus *why* sales contrast, in which focusing more on the *why* has been proven time and again to be the better option.

The more I spoke with members of the FOJ, the more I realized that their focus was on selling services to IT departments rather than selling products to improve learning. While most of them knew sales, they knew very little about education, which I also saw as a problem. Refreshingly, there was one exception. Jim had delegated the sales operation role to a man named Mike Thornberry, who was a seasoned Apple employee with good ideas which, unfortunately, Jim tended to ignore. Like the rest of Jim's soldiers, Mike was expected to simply follow orders, not offer up ideas. It reminded me of a quote by Master Chief John Urgayle in the war movie, *G.I. Jane*, "When I want your opinion, I'll give it to you."

It became clear to me early on in my visit that the main cause of Apple Education's sales problem was due to the Atlanta office culture that Jim had created and controlled. Being based out of Atlanta instead of Cupertino intensified the problem, because it ensured that new sales employees were either unaware of what Apple's culture was, or they were simply allowed to ignore it altogether. But having a misaligned culture wasn't the *only* problem.

It turned out that Jim had been developing and selling applications that his team developed locally. But Steve had made it clear that all Apple software must be developed, tested and approved by Apple's official software engineering team. He had prohibited software development in the field primarily to ensure that Apple computers remained free from bugs, viruses, and incompatibility issues. He knew that a single software mistake could hurt Apple's carefully crafted brand. Jim didn't seem too concerned about any of that though. In spite of Steve's directive, the FOJs followed orders and simply developed the education applications Jim wanted with no questions asked. FOJs were so emboldened in their efforts that I was even shown one of the software packages they had developed, which they were actively promising to customers in sales pitches. I saw and heard so many things that were clear violations of Apple guidelines that it became crystal clear why Jim had set up shop in Atlanta, 2,500 miles away from Steve and Cupertino: "Out of sight, out of mind."

TIME FOR A CHANGE

I knew the software development issue would be a lot easier to fix than changing the office culture, so I decided to first focus primarily on the former. I sat with Jim in his office and explained the situation while offering suggestions on ways he could achieve even better sales results that were within Apple's education goals. But rather than being appreciative and trying to work with me, he just stared blankly at me as if I were just wasting his time. Whenever I would stop talking to get a response, he would just nod his head and say things like, "Hmm, okay," "I see," and "Sure, sure." They were the kinds of responses someone might give to a pesky salesman while waiting for them to shut up and leave. Jim was not used to being told what to do by *anyone*, much less some newly appointed VP whom he viewed as little more than the new kid on the block trying to take control.

On my flight back to California I couldn't stop thinking about the Atlanta situation. I knew Jim would be a tough nut to crack, but if I couldn't even convince him to stop developing and selling his own software and services, my chance of getting him to try and change his entire office culture was next to none. I was beginning to think that Steve's prediction that I would end up firing Jim within a year may end up coming true. My Leadership by Vision model could accomplish a lot, but even it wouldn't be able to convince a stubborn VP to rethink and rebuild his entire culture, especially one who felt immune because of his relationship with our COO.

Days after returning to Cupertino, Tim Cook asked me to prepare an education presentation for an upcoming business review. Still new to the job, I didn't have all of the sales data I needed to make a thorough presentation, so I was going to need to rely on Jim. I had heard that he was a great presenter and a real showman, who had received big kudos in previous meetings by giving over-the-top presentations, which included things as wild as blowing up competitors' computers. I hoped that by Jim and me doing the presentation together, it might even open the door for a better relationship between us, thereby making it easier to get him on board with Steve's vision for Apple. I called and asked Jim to come to California and jointly make the presentation with me and asked him to send over the latest sales numbers and forecasts in the meantime. He agreed to both and I was already feeling like things were looking up.

But by the following week, now less than 24 hours from our meeting with Tim, I had not heard a word from Jim. He wasn't answering his phone, nor had I been sent any sales figures, goals, forecasts, or any other relevant information. Not surprisingly, his FOJ team claimed to not know anything and all just referred me back to Jim. I ended up camping out in a conference room all night, covering the walls with slides from my pending strategy plan, but I was still missing a lot of key sales data. Not knowing whether Jim had arrived from Atlanta yet (or if he was coming at all), I decided to call Mike Thornberry and asked him for help. He was unaware that a sales presentation was even scheduled, because Jim never bothered to mention it. Mike didn't have all of the data that Jim agreed to provide but did agree to help. Mike joined me the next day and we spent most of the day, until midnight, trying to fill in sales gaps and preparing the best we could in the event that Jim was a no-show.

The meeting with Tim began early the next morning. Just as everyone began taking their seats, Jim casually rolled in as if he didn't have a care in the world. Despite the fact that he was Apple Education's VP of "Sales," he had not bothered to bring along any sales numbers or forecasts, so throughout the meeting he just leaned back in his chair and quietly watched. When our turn came to present, Mike and I did the best we could with such a limited amount of information and so little sleep. The meeting went okay, but certainly did not live up to the standards that I had set for myself, especially considering it was my first presentation directly to Tim. But I had had it with Jim and had once again realized that Steve was right.

"I need to make a change," I told Tim the next day.

Even though I knew Tim was the one who hired Jim and had supported him over the years, I also knew there was no way I would be successful with him running his own service and product development group from what amounted to his own sales division in Atlanta.

"Are you sure?" Tim asked. "Because Jim is highly regarded and got the closest thing to a standing ovation at the last 'Top 100' meeting."

"Absolutely!" I insisted.

Tim considered a moment and then asked me to sleep on it. That night I tried to sleep on it, but I was still angry at the way Jim had been so carefree about his actions and could barely sleep. The next day I returned to Tim's office and confirmed my position. He sat silently for a moment, contemplating, then said, "Okay."

Since Jim was still in town, I called him into my office and broke the news, telling him the specific reasons for letting him go. When I finished explaining he sat quietly, staring, for what seemed like an eternity as I waited for a response. Finally, Jim said flatly, "No." I had no idea how to reply to that. I assumed he was refusing to accept my decision and perhaps challenging my authority altogether.

"I'm really sorry," I told him.

He was fuming. "I'll bet you are. We'll just see what Tim has to say about this," he said as he stormed out of my office.

To be clear, Jim had quite a bit of influence at Apple, even in Cupertino. Given Tim's obvious lack of enthusiasm for letting him go and the close ties the two had over the years, I wasn't sure what would happen next. Jim was certainly a lot closer to Tim than I was at the time and had even helped him learn about sales back when he was strictly an operation's expert. Also, every time Jim needed more money for a new idea he was pursuing, Tim would rarely ever turn down his request. It was due to that close relationship that Jim was now playing his "Tim card." Surprisingly, neither Steve, nor any other vice president that I was aware of, stood up to support my decision, but to his credit, Tim backed me up and reaffirmed that Jim was out. And while I had also worried that firing Jim might upset some of my colleagues, that soon became moot, because once Jim was gone, a number of VPs told me privately that I had made the right decision.

After Jim's departure, I assumed that the Vice President of Education Marketing, who had always been at odds with Jim, would welcome the news since she would now be able to work *together* with whomever took his place. But when I told her, she had some surprising news of her own for me. Back in March 2001, she had announced, with Steve's approval, that Apple was buying PowerSchool, Inc., the leading provider of web-based student information systems for K-12 schools and districts. But once the purchase was finalized, numerous scalability issues arose at several large installations. Steve realized he needed someone competent to fix the situation and decided it should be her. "You convinced me to buy PowerSchool," she told me Steve said to her. "Now go run it and make it work."

It was a good opportunity for her, but for me it meant that overnight I now had two huge openings to fill in the education division because, just like that, both my Vice President of Sales and my Vice President of Marketing were now gone. To make matters worse, I was expected to present my *entire* education strategy at an offsite Apple "Top 100" event that was just a month away. Fortunately, even though I was lacking both vice presidents, I still had some key staff members that I could lean on who included Paul Papageorge from Marketing, Bill Sutherland from Finance, and Mike Thornberry, Jim's Director of Sales Operations. I cannot stress just how valuable their help was to my early success this time around.

TOP 100 PRESENTATION

Most large companies are organized by division, run by division leaders, who typically spend their time focused on things happening with their own products. But this structure leaves these managers little time, or incentive, to know what's going on in other key divisions within their company. This lack of communication often leads to divisions operating in their own bubbles, often on different pages, and not knowing what else is going on throughout the company. It was this lack of company-wide communication that Steve had wanted to avoid, which is what led him to bring back. Another way Steve ensured that Apple leaders stayed on the same page was by holding annual executive retreats, which were called "Top 100s." Participants were invited by Steve and consisted of employees he viewed as the absolute best leaders at Apple, at least in terms of being able to realize his vision. It was during these gatherings that a number of executives in attendance would present the current status and future direction of the products they were responsible for.

What made Steve's "Top 100" presentations special was that they focused primarily on the products or services of the future, rather than just reporting on past and current business, which is what was expected of us at other meetings. Steve felt that it was imperative for all of us, as a group, to see the direction Apple was investing in so that we could better align our product directions with Apple's overall vision. All of Steve's meetings, even beyond the "Top 100," gatherings, always had a very clear purpose. For as long as I knew him, he felt that most meetings were a waste of time, unlike some execs who would hold meetings about *other* meetings!

I would be invited to Apple's "Top 100" meetings for the next fourteen years, but first I needed to survive my first one. It was not easy managing day-to-day tactical issues while simultaneously preparing a presentation on what I felt that Apple's role should be in the future of education. This was especially true given that we were expected to *invent* the future, not forecast it. Having to do this in front of the top 100 people in the company only increased the pressure on me to get it right. But since I was now without sales and marketing vice presidents, I was limited in the amount of quantitative data I would be able to present. Even so, I was able to share my overall vision on where I believed education needed to go and exactly what it was that Apple needed to do to lead the way.

During that first presentation I showed that Apple Education, as well as our competitors, was doing things backward. Up to this point, I explained, Apple had been creating consumer products and trying to find a place for them to fit in the education market. Instead, I argued, if we wanted to grow the education business, we needed to better understand the challenge of each stakeholder (administrators, teachers, students and parents) and aim our products toward meeting their needs. In other words, we shouldn't be designing and building solutions and then searching for problems they can fix, we needed to identify *specific* education challenges first and then design and build our products that would directly address them. Shifting our focus to learning, rather than just selling "boxes" was the key to Apple growing market share and increasing revenue, I argued. They agreed and, just as I predicted, after we started thinking in terms of learning first, our sales began to increase.

One of the best examples of this happened years later, after the release of the iPad. I gave a presentation to the Toronto Public Schools in Canada and afterward the superintendent came up to me and said, "You know, you're the first company that talks about learning, everyone else just wants to sell us boxes." We continued to chat about the learning process and at one point she said, "I've got a real problem with a high percentage of elementary school students who are not reading by fourth grade. Will you return and give your presentation to all of my kindergarten and first grade teachers?" Two weeks later she introduced me, not as an Apple vice president, but as someone who honestly cared about learning. I was then happily surprised when all of the 1,000 teachers in attendance raised their iPads and cheered loudly. It turned out that the superintendent had ended up buying iPads for every teacher, all based on Apple's learning focus and the ability to use our technology to directly address the district's reading challenges.

That incident would become a special moment for me but, in the meantime, I needed to make a convincing argument to Steve and my peers about what it was we needed to do to reinvent education, how we were going to do it, and why it was so important that we do it that way. What I lacked in numbers and statistics during my presentation, I tried to make up for by "thinking different" and offered a number of creative solutions. I was thrilled to hear afterward that almost everyone in the room understood and agreed. Most important, my ideas were able to get Steve's blessing, although I did have to promise him specific details on how I was going to make it all happen. I knew exactly what needed to be done, now it was just a matter of finding strong leaders for both sales and marketing.

THE SALES ANIMAL

If I was going to bring to fruition my ambitious plans to revamp education, I couldn't do it alone. A new VP of Sales would also have to understand that Apple was very different from other organizations. Even the best salesperson in the world would not survive there unless he or she understood and accepted our nontraditional culture. This meant that my VP needed to be willing and able to shake up the status quo across our entire sales division. A traditional sales leader would never have a chance of succeeding, I knew, what I needed was a *sales animal.*

In late 2002, at Tim Cook's suggestion, I met with a burly Englishman named Barry Wright about potentially coming on board and overseeing education sales at Apple. One of the first things I look for when hiring a salesperson is their ability to sell themselves for the position. Barry turned out to be a real character and wasted no time selling me on the fact that he was the right person for the job. He was a tough, proud man and, like me, he had enough energy to light up an entire city.

I went over Apple Education's strategic plan and explained in detail how and why our primary priority would be to provide teachers and students with the tools they needed to maximize students' potential in an ever-increasing digital world. I knew our products were better at doing this than other products available, but the trick was convincing traditional educational leaders to embrace change and "think different." Barry not only agreed with our philosophy but was highly enthusiastic and even shared some ideas of his own, which I appreciated.

I have always believed that there are three things required to successfully sell products in the modern-day education market. The first, as previously mentioned, is the ability to focus on the why over the what. Second is the understanding of the complexities of educational politics and purchasing decisions. Third is the ability to motivate both buyers (potential customers) and sellers (your sales force). I could tell from my very first meeting with Barry that he had all of this in spades and so, in late 2002, I hired him as Apple's Vice President of Education Sales. I would often use a fishing metaphor to describe our working relationship. I would lead the customers to the Apple boat with the message of transforming teaching and learning, and Barry would haul them in. I knew I had made the right decision, but I didn't know at the time just how much of a sales animal he would turn out to be.

I told Barry that the first things he would need to do were properly train our salespeople and increase the size of our sales force. He assured me that neither of those would be a problem and off he went. Unlike his predecessor, Barry turned out to be a great fit. He understood our culture, and got along well with Mike Thornberry, the rising operations star Jim had refused to let shine. Under Barry's leadership, Mike became an incredible leader himself and together the two of them became unstoppable, quickly transforming our sales department into a sales juggernaut of 700+ people.

Barry would go on to become a larger-than-life personality at Apple and was a great fit among the rest of us because he always thought big. One of the first things he did as Sales VP was to announce that he wanted to arrange a massive conference that our sales and marketing teams would attend along with a number of education experts from across the country. Even though it was already November, Barry insisted the entire conference be planned, set up, and take place by the end of February, a task that nearly everyone in our division thought impossible. It really was an outrageous goal, but no more so than Apple execs were used to hearing from Steve, who would challenge us to do the impossible on a weekly basis. Not surprisingly, no one who ever lasted at Apple told Steve Jobs that something was impossible.

In that same tradition, Barry was now insisting that his massive conference be up and going in just twelve weeks. I've always felt that passion is contagious, and Barry confirmed it by easily convincing his entire team that not only was this conference possible, but that it wouldn't even be difficult to do. Sure enough, thanks to the leadership of Barry and Mike Thornberry, by the end of February 2003 our multi-day sales conference kicked off in San Jose, California.

THE SALES TALK

I eagerly attended Barry's first sales conference, along with Steve and several other top executives. We were all impressed by how quickly and professionally it had been organized, but over the first few days it did seem a bit traditional. When I learned that Barry had scheduled a "sales talk" for the last day of the conference, I showed up not expecting anything out of the ordinary. His talk started off pleasantly enough, with him expressing gratitude and even praise for his team. But then, seemingly out of nowhere, he dropped the proverbial hammer on them. His mood changed instantly, and he got so serious that it reminded me of how Bruce Banner, whenever he got angry, transformed into the Incredible Hulk. All I could do was watch as Barry's cordiality had simply vanished, replaced by a hulking madman, stalking up and down the aisles, fire in his eyes, bellowing through a headset and wireless mic that were connected to booming speakers. "Don't be f*n losers!" he shouted with a beet-red face and sweat pouring off of him. "Not anymore!" I was in shock. Barry was always charismatic and passionate, but *this* Barry was downright scary.

As he continued his so-called "sales talk," I watched as his managers and sales team looked at one another, not sure whether to clap or cry. Barry stared coldly at every salesperson he walked by, explaining how, from that moment forward, every one of them would have dramatically increased expectations and excuses would not be tolerated. He said that what we were trying to do was bigger than Apple and that every student in the world was depending on each of them to bring education into the twenty-first century. Barry insisted that his sales team had better start making every sale a *personal* experience and if even one of them failed, the entire team would be held accountable. For the sales animal failure was not an option, not for him, nor for any member of his team. His message was clear: Future generations of students were depending on them, *personally,* to succeed and they had better not fail them.

Barry had turned what would otherwise have been a normal sales retreat into what amounted to a full-blown pep rally. The more he talked the more energy filled the room. Most of our sales force began cheering loudly whenever he would make a key point, while a few slumped in their seats, literally shaking with fear. Things would no longer be business as usual and it was visibly clear who was likely to succeed at Apple and who would struggle.

I recently had a conversation about Barry with Steve Wozniak's wife, Janet, who had worked for me for ten years in Apple's Education division. I told her that I was writing a book which would include a section describing Barry's infamous sales talk and asked for her own memories of the event. She described the relationship between Barry and me as being equivalent to the classic good cop, bad cop metaphor. "I remember that you spoke first and you were very passionate in a way that motivated us to believe we could change the world," she told me. "But then it was Barry's turn to talk and, oh boy."

Janet then recalled hearing Barry's thick Cockney accent and how he talked about growing up in a rough part of London where street fights were common, and how those experiences instilled in him the instincts of a die-hard fighter. She further recalled Barry walking up and down the middle aisle cursing, telling us how worthless we were, that what we were missing was the killer mentality he had, and that we needed to toughen up. Janet even remembered a specific quote from

Barry about our competition. "You need to fight them, kick them, bite them, get them down on the ground, put your foot on their throat and don't let up until you cut off their oxygen and they're dead!"

Janet and I agreed that one of the most disturbing moments of Barry's talk was when he began making what amounted to personal threats. He said he knew there were slackers at Apple, and that from now on he would personally "hunt them down" and fire them on the spot. He continued with this "insanity" for over 30 minutes, Janet recalled. She had heard enough, stood up and began to walk out, causing Barry to stop what he was saying mid-sentence and quietly watch her leave. "I'll never forget my regional manager, Judy Boggs, staring in horror as I made my way down the aisle while everyone else was afraid to move. Her eyes were just begging me to sit down," Janet said. "It was as if they were saying, 'Are you crazy?'"

Today, Janet and I look back and laugh at the whole thing, but it certainly wasn't funny at the time. Barry ended up always being like that in meetings with his team. He motivated through fear and intimidation and while some of that may have been off-the-cuff, he was a smart guy and I think much of it was a deliberate tactic that he knew worked. At the end of our conversation, Janet told me that once Barry saw that she was a hard worker who consistently produced, "He was really a cream puff and a super nice guy."

I understood that leaders motivate others in many different ways and any one of these ways have the potential to be successful. Barry's style was in stark contrast to my own, but it paid off because Apple's education business was about to go through the roof. During Barry Wright's tenure we ended up meeting our sales goals for 40 quarters in a row. When I first returned to Apple, the company's education sales hovered around $1 billion per year, but within ten years after I arrived and hired Barry, we were able to grow to over $9.5 billion. One of the main reasons for this growth was Apple's education division was now selling products based on *specific* learning needs rather than solutions in search of problems and were finally reaching the people who needed them most—teachers and students.

CHAPTER 11

APPLE EDUCATION

"Everyone has the sense that right now is one of those moments when we are influencing the future."

—STEVE JOBS

Steve Jobs had little formal education beyond high school and was fundamentally bored throughout his K-12 education. At around ten years old he came across his first computer and became fascinated. But it wasn't until years later, after he saw his first desktop computer at Hewlett-Packard, that he began to truly understand the potential computers had to reshape the future of education. From the moment I first joined Apple, he had already begun sharing with me his vision for computers in education, which mirrored one of his later public quotes: "I thought if there was just one computer in every school, some of the kids would find it and it will change their lives."

While there may not have been a VP of Education in the early days at Apple, education had always been seen as one of Apple's priorities and, as Steve put it, "part of Apple's DNA." Soon after I began in my role as Director of New Products, I was told by Steve that one of Apple's primary goals was to get creative technology into the hands of students. Like him, I knew the influence it could have on kids, mostly because of the effect it had on my own son, Kris, after Steve had brought that Apple II to my house. Steve and I both knew that it was never a question of whether or not personal computers could bring out a child's natural creativity and improve their motivation to learn, because we knew they could easily do both. The question we had was, *"How do we get them into their hands?"*

KIDS CAN'T WAIT

In 1978 Minnesota school kids were given access to five hundred Apple II computers through a deal Apple had made with the Minnesota Education Computing Consortium. Steve knew it wasn't enough and wanted to do more, but bureaucratic roadblocks had slowed the process to a crawl, frustrating him to no end. "We realized that a whole generation of kids were going to go through school before they even got their first computer," he later recalled. "But we thought—the kids can't wait." Steve believed that *all* kids needed to have access to computers, so that same year, he began an education marketing initiative at Apple called "The Kids Can't Wait." The stated goal of this new initiative was as simple as it was ambitious: to donate an Apple II to every school in America. The biggest problem was that Apple was in no position financially to accomplish such a massive undertaking. Luckily for us, a path opened up.

There was a federal law at the time that gave corporations a tax deduction if "a piece of scientific instrumentation or computer" was donated to a university for educational or research purposes. We felt that if we could get that law to cover K-12 schools as well, that would allow us to make nationwide donations. Steve flew to Washington, D.C. to lobby Congress and helped to get a bill submitted called H.R. 5573, aka the "Computer Equipment Contribution Act." Though the bill failed to make it out of committee, when political leaders in California learned of our effort, they agreed to implement "Kids Can't Wait" across the state's ten thousand schools, while giving us (as well as any other company) a tax break to help underwrite the cost of the program. Soon thereafter, personal computers began arriving at schools across California, giving thousands of students access to them for the first time. Steve would always refer to the program's success as being "phenomenal," and for the rest of his life he pointed to it as being one of the most incredible things Apple had ever done.

ST. MARY'S

Watching my son Kris play and learn on the Apple II, and later on a Lisa, I saw firsthand how much of an impact personal computers could have on kids. In February of 1979, I donated two Apple IIs to St Mary's, a K-8 Catholic school in Los Gatos, California, where Kris and my daughter, Tiffany, were attending. The school was thankful, but really had no idea what to do with the computers. They ended up cleaning out a janitorial closet, placing the computers in there and telling students they would be available to use before and after school, during free time, as well as at lunch and recess. Almost instantly the students became so interested in the computers that they swarmed the janitorial closet, and without any computer training whatsoever, managed to "figure things out" just by playing with them. One of the kids, I was told, was so motivated that he even learned how to read on them!

By the end of that school year, St. Mary's students voted the "janitorial closet" as their favorite class. The eighth grade graduating class ended up giving additional Apple IIs to the school as their class present, which was a nice gesture, but it also caused a bit of a dilemma. All of the computers would no longer fit in the closet, so after a bit of deliberation, the school decided to make "Computers" an official course for the following school year. I was excited about the news, at least until I saw their first exam, which was just the first page of the Apple II manual with some of the words left blank! All students had to do to pass the so-called "test" was to recall and write in the missing words, a ridiculous waste of technology. Shortly after that I wrote an article, "How the Apple was Lost on the Way to School," that warned if our educational institutions were not careful, they would end up changing Steve's vision of personal computers being "mental bicycles" to being "exercise bicycles" that never go anywhere.

ACOT RESEARCH

In 1986 Apple conducted a research project called Apple Classrooms of Tomorrow (ACOT). The project was a collaboration between Apple, public schools, universities, and research agencies. The goal was to study how the routine use of technology in classrooms might change teaching and learning and, if it could, to identify which specific models would bring about the most change. It was a well-done study that told us that kids learn best through active engagement and that computer technology was an effective form for engaging them. The results seem obvious now, but at the time it delivered a ton of insight and helped inform decisions that led to a large number of schools becoming more accepting of the use of educational technology in classrooms. By 2003 ACOT's findings were no longer helpful, which meant we needed more up-to-date research that would better inform our decisions regarding digital natives and twenty-first-century learning.

A year after the first iPhone's introduction, my education team began a long-overdue follow-up to ACOT called Apple Classrooms of Tomorrow—Today: Learning in the 21st Century, which we referred to as ACOT^2. Eventually we began a collaboration with Digital Promise, a well-known nonprofit that focused on ed tech and digital learning. ACOT²'s original leadership team consisted of Karen Cator, Marco Torres, Don Henderson, and Mark Nichols, Katie Morrow, and others.

Together, our goal was to figure out exactly what it would take to fully engage this new generation of students. The official description read, *"The intent of this second study was to identify the essential design principles for the 21ˢᵗ century high school by focusing on the relationships that matter most: those between students, teachers, and curriculum."* Whereas the original ACOT focused on whether or not technology could work in education, the focus of ACOT² was to find out how to make it work most effectively. The biggest takeaway from our ACOT² research was that all content needed to lead students toward becoming creators rather than just consumers. More specifically, classrooms needed to be creative, collaborative, relevant and challenging.

These findings, combined with key aspects from models like Bloom's Taxonomy, the TPACK (Technological Pedagogical Content Knowledge), and the SAMR (Substitution, Augmentation, Modification, and Redefinition, led us to develop a new pedagogy for learning that we called Challenge-based Learning (CBL). The model was designed to create collaborative learning experiences in which teachers and students worked together to study compelling issues, propose solutions to real-world problems, and take specific actions toward solving those problems. We weren't looking to invent something completely new with CBL. One of the key lessons I learned during my early years at Apple was that it's very difficult to get mainstream buy-in on something unless there's a sense of familiarity. This was one of the reasons that personal computers didn't take off until graphical-user interfaces were introduced with digital versions of familiar things like a desktop, files, and folders.

Even when novel ideas do catch on, they typically take years to implement and, in the education field, *decades*, if ever.

But we knew that "Kids Can't Wait," so rather than offer up a radically new learning model that no one understood, we wanted to apply innovation to an existing model that would greatly enhance its usefulness for twenty-first-century students. The model we used as a starting point was project-based learning (PBL), a popular hands-on learning pedagogy. We took the best parts of PBL and improved on it in many ways, most importantly by adding a technology component and the ability for students to choose their own, real-world projects. To spread the word, we turned to Apple Distinguished Educators, teachers whom we had recognized and rewarded for their effective use of technology in the classroom. With their help, backed up by the ACOT[2] findings, and supported by Digital Promise, CBL began to transform classrooms across the country.

THE BRAZIL PROJECT

The ACOT[2] research findings were central to our education strategy. It continued to shape pedagogies, not just at Apple, but throughout the United States and around the world. A good example of this was the Brazilian Project, which came together not long after Apple's decision to begin manufacturing in that country. Brazil's President had made it clear that if Apple wanted to have a manufacturing presence in the country, we had to invest in a research project that would help Brazil economically for the long term.

In response, Tim Cook's righthand man, Jeff Williams, came to us and asked for education-based ideas that might fit the bill. Brazil's President had been thinking in terms of our helping via manufacturing, but I suggested instead that we consider building up the country's nascent knowledge-worker economy by improving the ability for its citizens to code and build apps. We suggested that Apple could invest in a program within Brazil's universities that would train students, through challenge-based learning, in coding and app development. Brazil's leaders loved the idea. Once we were given the go-ahead from Apple, I chose my superstar technical contributor, Gordon Shutwik, to handle the program and logistics and, before long, the Brazil Project was up and running in ten universities across the country. It would go on to become incredibly successful. Students loved it because it taught them practical skills rather than theory, and even allowed them to start their own mobile app businesses before they graduated.

A few years after the program started, I attended an Apple developer conference at which a student entrepreneurship contest was being held and was excited to see one of the teams from the Brazil Project win first place. Over the next few years several more Brazilian students won too, causing executives at Apple and other big companies, to sit up and take note. I was especially happy to see some big tech companies like IBM begin to recruit students directly from Brazilian universities. Over time we continued to add more CBL-enhanced classes to the Brazil Project that included lessons on entrepreneurship and design thinking. It proved to be so successful that Apple went on to expand the project far beyond Brazil, starting similar programs in Italy, France, and Indonesia. I see this as a perfect example of how powerful it can be to put the right educational tools into the hands of students. In this case it not only boosted the career prospects of thousands of students, but also helped to boost the economy of the entire country.

STEVE'S VIEWS

Throughout the early 2000s, the "education reform" movement consisted of two very different schools of thought. Bill Gates, through his Bill and Melinda Gates Foundation, along with a host of politicians, consisting of both Democrats and Republicans believed that adding more standardized content and tests was the best way to improve educational outcomes for struggling students. This significantly flawed belief led to the federal Common Core Standards, a one-size-fits-all model that punished states, schools, teachers, and students who didn't perform up to "standard" on high-stakes tests. The other school of thought, which Steve and I fought for, was for more disruptive changes that relied less on memorization and testing and more on schools switching to innovative, individualized, and hands-on learning approaches.

Like everyone else, I have my own personal views when it comes to the more controversial topics in education, but as VP of Education at a company like Apple I didn't really have the luxury of sharing these views, because my job required public neutrality. Being in such a high-profile position of influence, I was commonly asked my viewpoints on virtually every controversial topic in education. But when a leader working for a large company takes a public stance on a controversial topic, it's automatically assumed that the company they work for feels the same way. In fact, when executives at the VP level and above at company's like Apple speak publicly, it's believed that they are *always* speaking as a representative of their company whether they mean to or not. This is why I had to always be careful about what I said and often had to bite my tongue in order to keep my mouth shut. Steve, on the other hand, could have cared less.

Everyone knows how passionate Steve was about Apple and the products he created, but many people don't realize how passionate he was about education. Most of the time when he talked publicly about education it usually related to technology and learning, topics that were not very controversial. But once in a while, someone would ask him about controversial issues related to education that had nothing to do with technology. Whenever that happened, I could be sure of two things. One, that he definitely had a very strong opinion about the topic, and two, that he was going to let everyone hear those opinions whether we liked them or not. Some of these topics included things like high stakes testing, letter grades, charter schools, school choice and vouchers, but for those who really wanted to really get Steve's blood boiling, they only needed to ask him about one thing: teacher unions.

TEACHER UNIONS

The only time I had ever flown with Steve on his private jet came just before an education conference in Plano, Texas. Typically, he would not attend these because he said it was "my job," but this was a special occasion because it was being sponsored by one of his biggest NeXt investors, billionaire Ross Perot. Steve told me that Ross had never missed a single NeXt board meeting and always had something positive to contribute, so he felt he owed it to him to support his conference.

Ross had always had an interest in various industries, which included both technology and education. This prompted him to host an ed tech conference where tech industry leaders would come together to discuss the role of technology in education. The most influential people he secured for this particular panel were Steve Jobs and Dell Computer CEO Michael Dell, two successful entrepreneurs with very different and highly opinionated views on education. The two men were sat right next to each other on stage, while I sat in the front row ready to be entertained by what was sure to be verbal fireworks. At first everything was congenial, and even humorous during some moments. But then the host turned to Steve and asked, "So, what's the biggest problem in public education today?"

Having asked such a broad, open-ended question, I had a feeling that I knew where Steve was going to take this, and I was right. "That's easy," Steve answered. "Teacher unions." *Uh oh*, I thought to myself, *here comes trouble*.

Before Steve even started explaining, he looked down at me from the stage and said, "John, I'm about to lose you some sales." He then began to blame unions for just about everything that's wrong with education. All I could do was watch and sweat, knowing that I was going to have some major cleaning up to do when this was over. The following day, Steve's strong union opinions made headlines that infuriated the teacher unions. And if the first time wasn't bad enough (for me anyway), a few days later Steve gave an interview with *PC World* in which he doubled down on his teacher union opinions.

Now I have no idea whether or not his *very* public opinions ended up losing me any sales, but they sure made for a painful trip to Washington, D.C. later that month when I was scheduled to meet with the teacher union presidents! I spent the better part of my time in that meeting just trying to convince them that Steve wasn't anti-teacher, he just felt they lacked the support needed from the unions who tended to be more political. But considering how publicly he had been making his views, my pitch that day was a tough sell.

Over the next several weeks, union leaders, teachers, and administrators began publicly painting a picture of Steve as a *radical* reformer and teacher-hater with an evil plan to replace classroom teachers with computers. It was all quite ridiculous, because while Steve did believe technology would transform education, he knew it could never be done effectively without the physical presence of a teacher. "I've helped put more computers in more schools than anybody else in the world and I'm absolutely convinced that is by no means the most important thing," Steve said in a 1995 interview. "The most important thing is a person. A person who incites your curiosity and feeds your curiosity; and machines cannot do that in the same way that people can." When I heard him say that I realized that Steve had just summed up my own motivation for following him back to Apple. As much as I loved the company, it was really the person leading it that incited and fed my own curiosity, and I was glad to be back.

CHAPTER 12

FOLLOW THE LEADER

*"Innovation distinguishes between a leader
and a follower."*

—STEVE JOBS

Throughout my second stint at Apple, I walked a thin line between reversing eight years of declining education revenues while also ensuring our education efforts were aligned with Apple's direction for the future. To ensure I was doing this properly I put a significant amount of time into understanding the areas in which Apple was currently investing its resources. Aside from the "Top 100" event, I made a point to ask other VPs a lot of questions, attend meetings, and learn everything I could about the company's hardware and software endeavors. I knew it was critical that the education strategic direction mapped to that of Apple's overall plan. What I learned was that, while Apple invested in multiple areas and products, the majority of spending was centered around four key segments: a new operating system (Mac OS X), creation application software (iLife suite, iTunes, and Pro apps), mobile devices, and retail stores.

MAC OS X

After Steve left Apple and started NeXT, he developed his own innovative NeXT computer. It was run by NeXTSTEP, an object-oriented operating system with a powerful and user-friendly interface. But the hardware components were quite expensive, forcing the price of the computer out of range for higher education, which had been Steve's key target market. Disappointed, he began looking into either selling the company or licensing out OPENSTEP, its proprietary software. It didn't take long to find a buyer because ironically, on February 4, 1997, it was Apple that ended up purchasing NeXT for $427 million, bringing Steve back to the company as an active board member. Now determined to turn around the financial misfortunes plaguing the company, he was cunningly and successfully able to oust Gil Amelio, the long-struggling CEO. Then, on September 16, 1997, Steve Jobs became Apple's interim-CEO—his first time ever officially leading Apple as its chief executive.

In his new leadership capacity as CEO, one of the first things Steve did was address the string of failed operating systems that Apple had developed. The new focus, he said, would be on the development of a new, modern version of Mac OS that used OPENSTEP as its foundation. The new system, Mac OS X, codenamed "Kodiak," was Unix-based, more powerful, and more reliable than what was on all other personal computers. On September 13, 2000, Mac OS X's public beta was released so that a select group of early adopters could test the software and report any bugs prior to the system's official release. The goal was to offer an OS that would entice software developers, such as Adobe, Microsoft, and others to develop applications that would run smoothly on the platform and thereby leverage the creative nature of the software development community, a lesson that had been learned early on with the Apple II.

On March 24, 2001, Mac OS X was officially released, becoming an instant hit and, unlike most of its predecessors, would go on to withstand the test of time. Subsequent upgrades to OS X were almost all named after big cats or places, including Cheetah, Puma, Jaguar, Panther, Tiger, Leopard, Snow Leopard, Lion, and Mountain Lion, Mavericks, Yosemite, El Capitan, Sierra, High Sierra, Mojave, and Catalina.

On my return to Apple the following year, Steve was still incredibly excited about the new operating system, telling me that he was "banking the entire company on OS X," and required that going forward, all future applications would *only* run on it. This instantly made OS X one of my four prime areas of focus. *What did this mean for Apple's education business?* I wondered. *How would I be able to leverage this new, widely praised system in ways that would help transform not just our education business but education as a whole?* These were some of the questions going through my mind, but one thing I didn't need to ask about was Steve's vision for the new OS in education. He had made that abundantly clear the moment I started: "I want computers running Mac OS X in every school in America."

I knew I would need to put some serious thought into how to best accomplish that goal in the K-12 market, but I did have an idea to help us conquer the university market. At the time, a majority of university IT departments were not supporting Macs. Not only was there limited student and faculty usage, but university IT workers had little familiarity with the Mac operating system, as they had been exclusively trained on Microsoft's platform. To begin solving this problem I did a quick study of university student expenditures and the individual market size (student and faculty) on campuses. I concluded that the best solution would be to focus on increasing the percentage of incoming freshmen who brought Macs to school with them. We ended up creating a "Back to School" promo each year where students were given a significant discount on Macs along with a free add-on, typically a piece of software and eventually an iPod. The promo was so successful that if one were to glance into university classrooms today, they would see most students seated behind an open MacBook.

X FOR TEACHERS

As our university program began taking off, it was time for me to figure out how to get Mac OS X into "every school in America" as Steve had envisioned. We both knew that OS X had game-changing potential for K-12 learning and I was excited to now be playing a lead role in making that happen. As I've said many times, all students possess a little bit of genius within them, but they often need the right tools to help bring it out. I knew that OS X was the perfect tool for this because it provided a reliable foundation for a variety of applications that could directly empower students' creativity. In order for this to work, however, schools had to actually have access to the OS. I did a study that found that only 6 percent of the Apple computers in the K-12 education market were even *capable* of running OS X!

When I told Steve about my findings, he arranged for us to sit down with Phil Schiller where the three of us could discuss possible solutions. It was during this meeting that we devised a marketing program that Phil Schiller named "X for Teachers." The idea was that Apple would give a free copy of Mac OS X to every teacher in North America, which we believed would then put pressure on schools and district IT departments to start taking us more seriously. Many of them had grown weary of Apple's obsolete and failed operating systems over the previous few years and had migrated to Microsoft. It was now my job to help them realize that, with Steve as CEO, there was a *new* Apple, and that from now on things were going to be very different. I knew our idea was solid, but the scale of such a program was unprecedented and implementing it ended up consuming my entire marketing budget for the year.

Aside from "X for Teachers" being such an expensive endeavor, I knew that I was also going to need technical help.

Upon my return to Apple, I had inherited a good team, but no one on it was technical, which meant that they couldn't tell me which features in OS X would be best able to empower education. Then one day I was in the cafeteria and ran into Gordon Shukwit, who had co-founded a successful tech start-up that was eventually bought by one of the companies I was advising in my venture capital days. I was surprised to see him now seeking employment at Apple, especially since we were in the midst of a hiring freeze. His expertise wasn't in education, but I knew he had the technical acumen required to successfully map key features of OS X to specific educational needs. Luckily, I was able to convince him to join my team, which turned out to be one of the best early moves I had made. I sent Gordon around the world observing education installations in order to better understand the learning needs of schools and how we could map those needs to OS X functions and the information he gathered proved to be indispensable.

Steve always said that "free" is a powerful word, but I also knew that giving something away for free doesn't guarantee that people will actually use it. But when it came to giving away Mac OS X, both Steve and I were highly optimistic. I remember meeting with a K-12 school's IT manager who told me how much pressure he had gotten from teachers and then showed me an email from one of them that read, "You made the transition from typewriters to computers and now Mac OS X is the best OS out there. So quit whining and start supporting it!" Well, we finally did, and the results were phenomenal. "So how many teachers do you think will take us up on the offer?" I recall asking Steve just before we launched the campaign. He thought about it a moment. "I don't know," he replied. "Probably around ten to fifteen thousand." Ultimately 500,000 teachers across North America took us up on our offer for a free copy of Mac OS X, showing that, as ambitious as he was, even he sometimes underestimated our success.

One of my most memorable moments from around this time happened when I received a pretty disheartening phone call from Steve. Not long after "X for Teachers" had launched and schools had begun installing OS X, he found the registration process gave customers the right to opt out of providing personal information. I was in a meeting at Harvard University when I received what appeared to be an urgent call from him. "What the f**k are you doing?" he yelled. I had no idea what he was talking about and was shocked because it was extremely rare for him to get so upset at me.

"What do you mean?" I asked.

He was furious.

"Why the hell are you allowing people to opt out of a *free* program?"

"Well, because it's the law," I countered.

There was silence on the other end of the line.

"Are you telling me I can break the law?" I asked.

"I, uh, well, uh.... I've got to go prepare for a board meeting. I'll get back to you."

I never heard anything else about it. Although the media constantly portrays Steve as being this ruthless dictator of a leader, the truth is he respected people who knew what they were talking about, could justify their decisions, and were willing to stand up to him when needed.

iLIFE

In the late eighteenth-century, German educationalist Friedrich Froebel found that the best way to promote learning in children was through play. His studies found that people are naturally creative, and that their creativity was best brought out inside educational environments that included materials (which he called "gifts") that encouraged learning through hands-on play. The idea was to teach young children through ways they valued and enjoyed rather than through ways they viewed as useless and boring. It was through this lens that I decided to focus part of my team's attention on ways we could build our own digital version of Froebel's tools for digital natives. I viewed technology as the twenty-first-century equivalent of Froebel's tools that had the ability to include various hands-on learning activities. One of the ways I knew we would be able to do this was through Apple's *iLife* software suite.

The iLife suite was a collection of software apps released by Apple in late 2002 that consisted of several key programs for creating, organizing, editing and publishing media. The suite included iMovie, iPhoto, iDVD, iWeb, and eventually Garage-Band. Most of these programs would eventually end up being pre-installed on Macbooks, but at this point they were being sold as a bundle. According to Bloom's taxonomy, the most influential model used to classify educational learning objectives, *creation* is a higher order skill, and I knew that each of the iLife apps gave students ways to create and learn simultaneously.

iMovie was a video creation and editing application in which users could easily create and edit their own professional-quality videos. Through the app, students were able to easily learn a valuable skill (even more so once YouTube's distribution channel was introduced a few years later) and use the videos they created to communicate their understanding of a topic in ways that were once reserved for Hollywood and Japanese corporations.

iPhoto allowed students to import, store, organize, edit and print photos in creative ways. The common maxim that a picture is worth a thousand words had never been truer in education now that students were trying so desperately to make sense of volumes of information. To be able to easily find, prepare, and implement photos in presentations made a huge difference for both students and teachers.

iDVD allowed students to customize their own DVD with tools such as backdrops, menus, slideshows, and home movies that could then be played on any DVD player. It was this last feature that my son, Jonathan, used to build his portfolio for a college application requirement at The Savannah School of Art and Design (SCAD), which subsequently earned him a scholarship.

iWeb was an app that allowed students to design, develop and publish their own blogs or websites without needing to know how to code, which was well timed because the World Wide Web was beginning to explode in popularity, giving anyone with access to a computer and modem the ability to publish in this new digital world.

Finally, in 2004, GarageBand was added to the iLife suite as an easy way for students to create and edit their own music, while also giving them the ability to add unique music to their videos. When combined with the other iLife applications, GarageBand, like Apple's other creative applications, gave students the ability to truly exhibit their talents. For example, students could now create and edit photos (iPhoto), use those photos in a video that they create and edit (iMovie), create and edit background music for it (GarageBand), port it to a custom DVD (iDVD), and finally, discuss, promote, and sell it on a website that they design and build (iWeb). It was the digital equivalent of a studio, stage and audience.

The more the creative learning potential of iLife became clearer to us, the more we shifted its focus specifically toward education, which ended up giving millions of students access to an important learning tool. The creative suite, which was also in line with Apple's popular genius campaign, ended up becoming a huge success and even winning a prestigious education award. For his part, Friedrich Froebel's ideas didn't do so bad either. He ended up merging his innovative tools and activities into specialized programs that operated out of centers for creative play referred to as *kindergarten.*

iTUNES

Aside from Mac OS X and iLife, another major software project going on at Apple when I arrived was iTunes, which itself had an interesting backstory. In June of 1999 a free file-sharing service for music was founded by entrepreneurs Shawn Fanning and Sean Parker that they called Napster. The platform provided one of the first ways for people to download MP3 files of individual songs. As word about such a unique service began to spread, its popularity exploded and within a year Napster found itself with over eighty million registered users from all over the world. But the problem was that it was illegal. It violated copyright protection laws on every song listed, which infuriated artists and music publishers who were not making a dime from their own music.

Napster software initially ran only on Windows, but in 2000 a Macintosh version of the service called "Macster" was released. While this second iteration had some success, it was nowhere near as much as Napster had enjoyed. As Steve, ever the opportunist, watched the success of these applications, he realized just how much of a demand there was for streaming music. It was these illegal file-sharing apps that paved the way for Apple's 2001 release of a similar, legal version in the form of an online store called iTunes.

iTunes offered hundreds of thousands of individual songs for 99 cents each, giving fans a way to purchase, sort and access their favorite songs without having to buy a full CD. I was intrigued by the app and knew that the iTunes model would continue to play a huge role in Apple's future, but at that time Apple was only using it as a music streaming and distribution platform. Not only did it have no other functionality, but it was also designed to work only on Macintosh, which I felt left out millions of potential users.

At first, I wasn't sure of the best ways to leverage iTunes in education. Even though "X for Teachers" helped bring Mac OS X into more classrooms, Macintosh computers themselves were still costly. This was a key challenge for us that limited the number of teachers that had access to "X for Teachers," even if we were giving it away for free. I knew that realistically, if technology was going to transform education, Apple needed to offer a line of more affordable products. Luckily, we already had a consumer product that was both affordable and fun.

iPODS

On October 23, 2001, a month after Macintosh's version of iTunes was released, Apple also released its highly anticipated music player, iPod. iPods were portable media players and precursors to the iPod Touch, iPhone, and iPad, although the latter two wouldn't be released for at least another six years. One of the most memorable moments in Apple's history came when Steve went on stage and introduced the iPod simply as "1,000 songs in your pocket." Such a small phrase, but in typical Steve fashion, he painted a picture with words that ingeniously captured the public's attention. iTunes became the software that ran on the iPod and made it work, essentially iPod's operating system, and was used to transfer music and other media from a computer to other compatible devices and vice versa. Unlike Sony's popular Walkman, which would play CDs in whatever order the songs happened to be in, iTunes allowed users to create individualized playlists and keep them synchronized between devices. By April of 2003, iTunes also included the iTunes Store, eliminating the need for users to buy

CDs and DVDs at physical stores, and allowing them to play songs and movies instantly.

Early on I began thinking of ways that iPods could be used in education. Unfortunately, they had been banned in most schools, likely because teachers knew that students would prefer listening to cool music over boring lectures. I believed iPods should have been considered as a platform for applications that went far beyond just music but before that could happen, I needed to prove it to Apple. In particular I wanted Steve to consider incorporating podcasting functionality into iPods so that I'd have something to pitch as an educational feature to schools.

So, I began thinking more about podcasting technology and the possibilities it could bring to education if it were more widely available. It was still in its infancy at the time and although it may not have been revolutionary, I felt that it had the potential to be if things like on-demand video, instant messaging, and interactive lessons were added to it. Eventually, iTunes U would add all of this functionality, but for now we were still just trying to figure it out.

During an educational conference in Philadelphia, members of my marketing team went along the historic Liberty Walk and captured content for a podcast we were creating. They recorded the tour guide speaking and took pictures of each landmark along the way. Upon their return to Apple, we wrote the code that would weave together the various photos and video into a single podcast. I took the finished podcast to our software engineers and explained how important it was that this type of functionality be available on iPods so that I could convince school administrators to allow, if not encourage, their use in schools. The engineers loved the idea and agreed that some form of this functionality needed to be available on the iPod, but were hesitant to include it as a stand-alone application.

Instead, they decided to add it as a capability in GarageBand, as part of the education-based iLife suite. It was exactly what I needed to convince schools to give iPods another look.

The proof came in early 2003 when Stephanie Hamilton, a member of our education marketing team, visited an elementary school in Alaska. She was walking around a fourth-grade classroom observing students at work when she ran across an indigenous girl updating a podcast she had posted in which she had described her native culture. Podcasting was defined at the time as "the practice of using the internet to make digital recordings of broadcasts that are available for downloading to a computer or mobile device." As Stephanie looked closer at the girl's work, she saw that this particular podcast had over 10,000 views. "Wow," Stephanie said. "That's a lot of views. You're famous!" Without so much as glancing up from her work, the girl replied, "Oh, that's so yesterday." Stephanie, herself a former teacher, couldn't believe how fast these kids were creating and posting unique content and how passionate they seemed to be about it. As she relayed this story to me, it reaffirmed how important it was for Apple to find ways to appeal to children's natural creative instincts.

iTUNES U

Since Apple's engineering team had supported my podcast idea by including the functionality in GarageBand, I felt empowered to continue to try and make the most out of iPod, and later iPhone, technology. I continued to see iTunes as being our best option to deliver lectures, curriculum, and books and believed in it so much that I added the idea to the end of my "Top 100" presentation. In it I had imagined a version of iTunes called iTunes U, where classrooms could instantly access educational videos, podcasts, software, and even specific curriculum and chapters of textbooks. iTunes U, I knew, had the potential to become an all-in-one distribution platform that could become a key supplement throughout the learning process.

When pitching the idea for iTunes U, I was fortunate that Eddy Cue, our VP of iTunes, was willing to go to bat for me and even agree to fund its development. So as not to alarm Steve, we decided not to mention it to him because we knew he would likely say no, having wanted to keep iTunes as strictly a music-based platform. But I felt that this was so important that this was one of those times when it's better to ask for forgiveness than permission. Steve would not learn about iTunes U until much later, during a phone call from the president of Stanford University, who told him how much the Stanford students loved it.

After the phone call, Steve began to recognize iTunes U as a digital distribution ecosystem in which devices of all kinds could use it as a platform for a vast number of programs, management tools, e-commerce, and especially education. He did, however, say that he "didn't want to wake up any sleeping giants," so in an effort to keep the program somewhat under wraps, he made the decision that we would not openly publicize it and instead rely on universities and students to spread the word organically.

It wasn't until May 30, 2007, that Apple officially announced the launch of our first iteration of iTunes U, offering anyone access to free content from top universities. Our press release at the time described it as "a dedicated area within the iTunes Store featuring free content such as course lectures, language lessons, lab demonstrations, and campus tours provided by top colleges and universities including Stanford University, UC Berkeley, Duke University and Michigan." Being able to collaborate with such elite colleges and universities was huge. It was the dream of hundreds of thousands of students to attend these universities even though only a handful are ever accepted. Now, iTunes U had stepped in, giving them a chance to experience and learn directly from these schools, in the comfort of their own home. For the first time, both entertainment *and* educational content could be loaded onto an iPod with a single click.

Within its first year, iTunes U ended up garnering over four million downloads. On November 4, 2007 *The Washington Post* columnist Jeffrey Selingo published a detailed article about the platform with the headline, "Is iTunes U for You?" in which he followed its use by Walter H.G. Lewin, an influential professor at MIT. Overnight, the article exposed millions of more people to the platform, greatly expanding its user base.

Throughout the early growth of iTunes U, podcasting technology steadily captured the attention of the tech industry but podcasting itself had not yet gone mainstream. In an effort to speed things up, I began trying to spread the word at conferences and trade shows. As one of the larger trade shows was about to start, I asked for a spot so that we could spread the word about podcasting. But the conference organizers turned me down, claiming that they were fully booked and that even if they weren't, they had never heard of podcasting anyway. I ended up talking them into letting us in, but the only available slot was at the same time as the opening cocktail party which, the organizers said, would leave us with no one left to attend our presentation. I told them that I'd take my chances. On the night of the event our presentation had so many people clamoring to learn more about iTunes U and podcasting that the fire department deemed it a hazard and locked the doors, prompting us to run a second session later that night. That was the moment I realized just how hot podcasting was going to be.

By all early measures iTunes U was a success, but it wasn't without its limitations. For example, much of the educational content the universities were producing was still in the form of monotone-delivered lectures, which have been proven time and again to be a highly inefficient mode for teaching and learning. There was also no way for iTunes U users to interact with professors or other students, a feature that I vigorously sought to include. Eventually, the iTunes group made the decision to separate the platform's audio from its video components. Audio podcasts were moved out of iTunes and into a standalone Podcasts app, and video content was moved into a standalone iTunes U app.

Having a dedicated iTunes U app was both good and bad. The good news was that the platform was upgraded to include more interactivity which allowed instructors to be much more involved in their students' work. But the cons were far worse than the pros. The biggest problem was that iTunes had already been available on all major OS platforms for years, so removing iTunes U from iTunes meant that iTunes U suddenly became available only on Apple devices, significantly limiting the number of people who could access it. This amounted to a virtual deathblow as universities suddenly stopped adding content. In 2017 the iTunes U app was discontinued and its content moved into the Podcasts app which, of course, was also exclusive to Apple products.

RETAIL STORES

Finally, the fourth major Apple investment I had identified early on was retail stores. In early 2001, just before Apple was about to launch its first physical store, retail VP Ron Johnson did something not a lot of people were brave enough to do—he told Steve Jobs he was wrong. This was not something we saw very often at Apple, and the unspoken rule was that if you chose to do so you better know what you're talking about and, just as importantly, you better have a solution that was better than his.

In this particular instance, Ron felt that the retail store layout that Steve had designed was all wrong and suggested that rather than organizing the store around our products, it needed to be organized around activities. After the suggestion, Steve considered it for a moment and then agreed that it was indeed a better idea. But Steve wanted to see it first and told Ron to build a model store in one of Apple's empty buildings on Bubb Road.

While most of us agreed that it was a good idea, some felt like it had come too late in the game, especially considering that Ron had to build a model store and the Apple Store's grand opening was right around the corner. Ron pulled it off quickly and showed his model store to Steve. The next day Steve made the shocking announcement to the leadership team that the store's grand opening was being postponed, and that Ron was to redesign it.

To Steve, doing things right was always more important than doing them fast, even though he was notorious for his unreasonable deadlines. Anyone who carefully looks at Apple's history will see that we were rarely ever the first to do *anything*. We didn't create the first computer, GUI, portable music player, music streaming service, mobile phone, tablet, or even the first smart watch. What we did, better than anyone else in the world, was recognize the full potential of technology that already existed, make products better than anyone could have imagined, and integrate them in ways that worked together flawlessly. In other words, we weren't inventors at Apple, we were *innovators*. "We're not going to be the first to the party," Steve once said in an interview. "But we're going to be the best."

Ron went on to successfully redesign the layout of the retail store and the grand opening took place in May of 2001.

That store ended up surpassing $1 billion in revenue each year in its first two years. The success of the store led Steve to announce he wanted Apple Stores opened all over the world and I knew for certain that retail was one of Apple's four major investments, in both time and money, for the foreseeable future.

I now needed to find ways to leverage the insane growth of these stores for education so, in late 2002, I approached Ron and suggested that we work together to include an educational aspect in our physical stores. Many people thought the idea was ridiculous, holding the traditional view that stores were for selling products, not teaching kids. But as I had been arguing throughout my entire time as VP of Education, in order to boost sales, we needed to first show people why our products mattered. This laser focus on *why* was the same argument I had made to Jim in Atlanta, to Steve at the "Top 100" meeting, to the Sales Animal, and to everyone else who would listen. Ron was extremely open-minded and supportive, and we came to the agreement that his retail division and my education division would partner up and develop what would become Apple's first in-store educational program—School Nights.

SCHOOL NIGHTS

Apple's School Nights was a program that gave students the opportunity to visit our retail stores at night and freely use our computers to do their homework, work on projects, create media, and design presentations. Students from all over the country were having fun and learning at the same time, a refreshing change of pace for most of them. To cap things off we invited their parents in to view and celebrate their digital work and it became a very special moment.

I vividly recall our very first School Night at which I found myself drawn to a fourth-grade girl with pigtails and a baseball cap flipped sideways. She had been working dutifully on a movie she was making on a Macintosh, but I couldn't help but wonder why she was making it in only a 2x2-inch square. "Don't you want to make that bigger?" I asked her. Without hesitation she shook her head and said, "No, I can't do that. Because if I make it larger it will start to pixelate." *Wow*, I thought, *she really knows her stuff.* "Also, the file would be too big to send to my partner school in Beijing," she added. I was impressed, but not surprised because this story is not unlike what happened with the Alaskan indigenous girl and her podcast, with my own son Kris and his Apple II, and with millions of other digital natives all over the world.

The School Nights program continued for the next several years and then morphed into something even better—Apple Camp, where kids could visit any Apple Store and receive free lessons on music creation, video editing, robotics, coding, and more. The demand for Apple Camp would grow such that every Apple Store ended up with waiting lists. In a sense, it became what amounted to a digital kindergarten, which I believe would have made Froebel proud.

CHAPTER 13

THE VISIONARY

*"If you are working on something exciting that you
really care about, you don't have to be pushed.
The vision pulls you."*

—STEVE JOBS

Steve Jobs is widely considered to be one of the greatest visionaries to have ever lived. The revolution he engineered in the personal computer industry was just the beginning of the various markets he either directly changed or indirectly influenced, including laptops, operating systems, software, music players, telephones, tablets, watches, and televisions. This list doesn't even include thousands more made possible by his creation of an app-based platform, and corresponding ecosystem (App Store) that has allowed hundreds of thousands of budding entrepreneurs to create and market their own businesses. If you were to factor in opportunities created by copycats, Steve's achievements become even more impressive. One could even make the argument that he was responsible for the widest variety of technological change in American history. He was the very definition of a visionary—someone with the ability and courage to envision, develop, and market a future that doesn't currently exist.

Sometimes people like Steve come across as prescient, lucky, or a little of both. When they succeed at changing the world they're seen as "visionaries" and "innovative geniuses," but when they get something wrong, as they all do at times, they are criticized for being overly optimistic, dreamers, or living in a so-called *reality distortion field*. This annoying little term, implying that Steve was out of touch with reality, has been tossed around quite a bit in the media. While it may have a cool-sounding name, the concept behind it is flawed. For one thing, just because something isn't real today, who's to say it won't or can't be real tomorrow? Also, just because something doesn't seem real to *you*, doesn't mean it's not real. "People can only perceive what they see," Ralph Waldo Emerson said. Like beauty, reality is also in the eye of the beholder.

When it came to vision, Steve excelled at predicting the direction the world would go with technology, usually well before that technology existed. His intuition was almost always spot on, and he surrounded himself with creative people, all capable of turning innovative ideas into final products. And if the future he envisioned didn't arrive as quickly as he had hoped, he would simply create it himself. This was not new. Steve had this gift of vision well before I met him. It's what guided him to start Apple with Woz in the first place and it was the reason he convinced me to leave HP and join his planned revolution.

While Steve's vision was usually spot-on, it was also dynamic. Its destination rarely changed, but the paths he would take to reach it constantly evolved as he learned. Unlike some visionaries throughout history, he was always willing to get out of his own bubble and would actively look to learn from others. I know Steve often came across to some as being an egomaniac, but, on the contrary, he seemed always ready to learn from anyone whom he felt had something to offer. Being open to and accepting Ron Johnson's retail store idea was a good example of this, but there were others. One lesser-known story I've found to be a particularly good example of him being influenced by someone *outside* of Apple began with a conversation he struck up with Fred Smith, the longtime CEO of FedEx.

We had known for some time that Steve had a tremendous amount of respect for "Freddy" and so it wasn't much of a surprise to hear that he had been inspired by something he had told him. The bigger surprise, for me at least, was the gravity of the topic that they were discussing. Freddy was trying to convince Steve that Apple should completely abandon its current strategy of shipping our products to several distribution centers around the United States. Instead, he suggested, we should start shipping our products directly from the manufacturing line to the consumer.

What Freddy was suggesting on that plane with Steve was no small adjustment, but rather a major change in Apple's business structure that, if instituted, would completely transform our business operations model. But after giving it a bit of thought, Steve agreed with Freddy and wasted no time telling all of us during an executive meeting that Apple was henceforth going to shut down *all* of our distribution lines and start shipping directly to customers from our manufacturing lines. We were all shocked. No one in the room saw this coming, especially those responsible for distribution oversight, who quickly realized they might be out of jobs. Some Apple executives quietly questioned the wisdom of Steve's decision at the time, but the move led to the creation of the Mac Factory which, over time, significantly improved our bottom line. Of course, with all that new shipping going on, FedEx didn't do so bad either.

MAJOR INFLUENCES

There have already been tons of books, shows, and articles touching on people who were said to have been major influences of Steve's. Some of the more commonly mentioned are Intel founder Robert Noyce, Oracle founder Larry Ellison, and just about everyone featured in Apple's Think Different campaign. The Steve I knew was always looking to meet and learn from those he respected, and he would frequently share with us the things he had learned from them. In my conversations with him, the three influencers he most talked about were Sony founder and former CEO Akio Morita, Hewlett-Packard co-founder Bill Hewlett and, especially when it came to creativity, Walt Disney.

Steve would often talk about how he met Akio Morita at Sony headquarters in Japan, how much he admired his business instincts, and how he was thrilled when he found out the feeling was mutual. He told us about how the revered Sony leader had even given him a personal tour of Sony and how, during subsequent visits to Japan, he would casually walk around Sony talking with employees. Over time the two leaders would grow to form a special bond that lasted right up to Akio's death in 1999 at the age of 78. The results of their bond could be seen well after Akio's death though, as Sony and Apple continued to maintain a solid working relationship and even worked on several major projects together. I wasn't privy to the specifics of Steve and Akio's relationship, but I do know that Steve was fascinated by the way the elder leader built and ran Sony, because it had a big influence on the way Steve built and ran Apple.

The second major influence on Steve was my old boss at HP, Bill Hewlett. In the early days at Apple, Bill seemed to me to be the one who had the most direct influence on him. It was Bill who Steve cold-called as a teenager and asked for spare computer parts and who gave him his first job as an intern building frequency counters on an HP assembly line. After I joined Apple, Steve asked if I would introduce him to Bill and I quickly set up a meeting. During the meeting I'll never forget how honored I was, and how lucky I felt, walking into Bill's office, introducing two of the men I most respected. The meeting was a big deal to Steve because he had never met Bill face to face, having only talked to him on the phone. At one point I relayed to him the last meeting I had with Bill, at which he shared with me an important business lesson, "More companies fail from indigestion than starvation." In other words, the key to survival was to keep things as simple and defined as possible and to never take on more than is required. Steve took this philosophy to heart throughout his time at Apple. Years later Steve would be widely quoted for relaying his own variation of it: "I am just as proud of the eight projects we don't do, as the two that we do."

The main reason I believe Steve is still considered to have been such a remarkable visionary is how creative he was and his innate ability to think outside the box. Who most inspired his creativity is a matter of debate, but I know for certain that one key person was the legendary animator and founder, Walt Disney. Whenever Steve wanted to make a point involving creativity, he would often talk about and quote Walt, to me privately and during Apple's weekly executive meetings. At one of these meetings, Steve was asked about his thoughts on Microsoft blatantly copying nearly everything we were doing at the time. His response was to share with us one of his favorite Walt Disney quotes. Whenever Walt was asked his feelings on copycat artists, he would respond, "If I spend my time worrying about that, I won't have time to be innovative!"

Walt was around long before Steve's time, but it always felt to me that Steve believed in some small way that he might be able to channel some of Walt's creativity as he designed Apple products. I also believe that Steve's admiration for Walt was a key factor in his decision to sell Pixar to The Walt Disney Company, a move that made him Disney's largest individual shareholder and put him directly inside the house that Walt built.

VERBAL ANIMATION

While Steve never aspired to be an animator like Walt Disney, he had long been a master of painting pictures with words, or what I call *verbal* animation. He had an uncanny ability to inspire all of us through his creative use of words. He would always rely heavily on metaphors, analogies, surprise and dramatic storytelling in ways that would simplify even the most complex concepts. I recognized this ability in him from the moment he shared with me the mental bicycle metaphor that had been inspired by the *Scientific American* article.

Another example of Steve's verbal animation was the first time he introduced the world to the iPod. He didn't start by explaining the ins and outs of music technology or the unique specifications of the iPod. Instead, he simply said that this tiny device would put "1,000 songs in your pocket." Short, sweet, and simple. He did this sort of thing during nearly all of his keynote speeches and really anytime he needed to explain a complex idea or question. He just had a knack for presenting, whether it was to a dozen employees in a staff meeting, a thousand students at a commencement address, or a million viewers watching him introduce a new product.

One of my favorite stories highlighting Steve's verbal animation skills took place in 1983 at Stanford University where the two of us were hosting what we called "brown bag lunches." In order to spread the word about Apple and scout for talent at the same time, we would set up stools inside one of the school's lecture halls. Students would bring their lunches in brown paper bags and eat while asking us anything they wanted to know about Apple. During one of these visits a student asked us what type of person Apple was looking to hire. My analytical mind instantly began thinking about things like "someone with an engineering or computer science degree," or maybe "someone with an MBA if it's for a marketing position." But before I could open my mouth, Steve said, "Think of an ice cream sundae." I looked over at him, trying to figure out where the heck this was going. "It's not the two scoops of vanilla ice cream that make the difference," he continued. "It's not the chocolate syrup or the whipped cream either. In fact, it's not even the cherry." Then came a long pause. I had no idea what he was talking about.

"You know what it is?" he finally said. "It's the few nuts on top. That's what we're looking for at Apple, we're looking for those few nuts that stand out, that add value to the sundae." In other words, not only were we looking for the best people at Apple, but they also needed to be nutty enough to *think different*. The sundae metaphor instantly painted a picture in the minds of the students who suddenly all wanted to work for Apple. Because of his deftness at verbal animation, Steve never needed a lot of words to make a point, just the right ones.

MARKET RESEARCH

Another example of Steve's verbal animation occurred frequently during our executive marketing meetings. He never paid attention to market research and would rarely ever hire outside consultants. There were several times I recall him quoting Bill Hewlett as saying, "Market research is only valid when evaluating existing markets." His point was that while this type of research may be good at analyzing current markets, they're virtually useless for those of us attempting to create new ones. This isn't to say we didn't do research, it's just a matter of the kind. Traditional market research asks people what they think they *want* and tells company's what products to design and build to meet that demand. On the contrary, Steve paid little attention to what people wanted, choosing instead to focus on what he believed they *needed*, whether they knew it or not. This was not unlike Henry Ford's theory mentioned earlier about why, when he was building his cars, he never asked the public what they wanted. "Because they would have just said a faster horse!"

This kind of thinking was constantly drilled into the brains of Apple executives, so Steve was not pleased when one of us referenced market research findings. In a not-so-subtle manner he would remind us that our energy should instead be focused on creating all new markets. One of the ways he used to illustrate this point was through a dartboard analogy. Instead of drawing concentric circles and then throwing a dart at the bullseye, he would throw the dart *first*, point to it and say, "This is us." He would then draw concentric circles around the dart and say, "Our competitors can throw next."

VISIONARY GAP

While Steve seemed to relish the idea of being an innovator and creative visionary, I think he realized that such a role also came with several downsides. One was that incredibly high expectations were always placed on him to get things right. Even the slightest public misstep would result in, often unfair, thrashings by both competitors and the media. The implication was that "geniuses" are supposed to be smart, and smart people don't do dumb things, therefore if they do dumb things, then perhaps they were never geniuses at all. This is a common, incredibly wrong, association fallacy, not to mention being just plain stupid. The truth is that geniuses get things wrong all the time and I would go so far as to say that doing so is virtually a *requirement*. One of my favorite quotes on this comes from Thomas Edison who, along with Einstein, was one of the smartest people to have ever lived. Edison said, "I have not failed. I've just found 10,000 ways that won't work." Fortunately, the Steve I knew never really cared what people thought about him or whether or not they agreed with, or even liked, his ideas. In his mind history would be the only judge that mattered.

Another challenge that Steve had was that he would think much farther out than others, who were often unable to keep up. This happened a lot during conversations in which he would appear to be operating in a different reality than the person he was talking to. He would continue to talk to them, assuming that they understood him because what he was saying just seemed so obvious. Not wanting to look like an idiot, the person he was talking to would just smile and nod in an attempt to hide their confusion. But that would turn into a one-sided conversation, which didn't appeal to Steve, who was more interested in getting as much out of a conversation as he gave. This *visionary gap* was frustrating for him and when that frustration merged with his notorious lack of patience, it sometimes got ugly, which then led to negative media coverage.

Over the years, Steve has gotten a bad rap as being the kind of boss who would always yell and scream and humiliate his employees to the point of tears. These portrayals make for good press, but to say they are exaggerated would be an understatement. He was opinionated, sometimes rude, and definitely impatient, especially when it came to people who he felt either weren't doing their jobs or didn't know what they were talking about. Steve had what I refer to as a "low tolerance for fools." What might have come across to outsiders as him being "mean" was actually him being extremely blunt. He was never afraid to say exactly how he felt and believed that doing so was the best and fastest way to get across the intense passion he had for whatever it was he was doing. It's the same reason people curse—it's a powerful way to emphasize what we're trying to say, even if that means being a bit belligerent. But despite the rumors, I don't recall Steve ever really *screaming* at us, mostly because he didn't need to.

The reason he didn't have to was that all of us had an enormous amount of respect for him, so knowing that he'd be disappointed in something we said or did (or didn't do) was enough to keep us on our toes. Blunt candor was typical of Steve but was never meant to be demeaning. I think he summed it up best when he was asked about it in an interview: "I'm brutally honest, because the price of admission to being in the room with me is I get to tell you you're full of shit if you're full of shit, and you get to say to me I'm full of shit, and we have some rip-roaring fights." He went on to talk about how this weeded out the B player "bozos" from the smart A players, and how "the people who do survive [at Apple] say that 'this was the greatest ride I've ever had, and I wouldn't give it up for anything.'" I could not agree more.

PATIENCE LEVEL

Another reason why I think Steve was always so blunt had to do with trust. As much of a marketing guru as he was, he never really trusted salespeople or anyone else with an agenda that he didn't recognize, agree on, or identify with. People who dealt with him both professionally and personally came to quickly realize that he simply could not be bullshitted. I learned this on my very first day at Apple when Steve sat barefoot on that table, inspecting the printer in front of its salesman and saying, "This is a piece of shit," before tossing it aside. At the time I got the feeling that Steve had not only hated the product, but also took it as a sign of disrespect that they tried to sell it to him in the first place. I felt that, in Steve's mind, the makers of the product *must* have known that it wasn't high quality and yet still attempted to sell it to him. If he viewed this as blatant deception and a slap in the face, then he was going to call them out on it and slap back.

Steve also hated excuses. He always challenged us to do better and believed strongly that if something was important enough, then we'd find a way. In meetings whenever one of Apple's executives didn't do something that Steve had expected to be done, he would ask why, and if that answer came in the form of an excuse, he would call them out on the spot without a shred of sympathy. During one of our marketing executive meetings, I remember someone being mid-excuse when Steve cut him off. "You know," he said. "When I came into my office this morning, I noticed my garbage had not been emptied, so I called and asked the janitor why it had not been emptied. He told me he was never given a key to my office." Steve looked silently around the room at us for what seemed like an eternity. We were all confused, unsure where he was going with this. "The *janitor* can have an excuse, but all of you don't have that luxury! You are all *vice presidents* and are not allowed excuses." We got the point loud and clear.

Another thing Steve didn't allow were prolonged presentations or explanations trying to justify something that we were doing. "People who know what they're talking about don't need PowerPoint," he would tell us. Everyone of us at Apple knew that if you were going to attend a meeting that Steve was in, then you sure as hell better know what you're talking about and be able to explain it in less than a minute or you're toast. He was notorious for not just interrupting but completely taking over subpar presentations, instructing the person giving them to just sit down and shut up. The fact was that Apple was always a fast-moving company and those Steve felt couldn't keep up were quickly moved aside.

STANDING UP TO STEVE

Most of us at Apple knew that, in Steve's mind, everyone was either a genius or an idiot and that he saw little space between the two. But he also believed that someone could be both of these things at different times. He would even admit once in a while that he had been wrong about someone being an idiot at all. This did not happen very often. When it did, it would almost always come after someone who knew what they were talking about had the courage to stand up to him. Make no mistake, standing up to him was not an easy thing to do. When doing so, we had to be *very* confident in what we were saying if we wanted to continue working for him.

I already shared one example of successfully standing up to Steve, when Ron Johnson argued that the Apple Store needed to be redesigned and Steve agreed. However, a more personal example happened in Apple's early days, not long after I had hired a young lady to manage the training operation for the introduction of Lisa. One day Steve ran into her and asked what she was doing. Whatever occurred in that conversation prompted him to call me at 2:00 AM, insisting that I fire her. But she was a good employee and a good person, and I had no reason to fire her. I told Steve that she was a great worker, that she worked for me, and if he wanted to fire her, he should fire me first and then go fire her. He fell silent for a moment and then hung up on me. A few months later he called me to brag about the same lady being such a great training manager. I laughed and quickly reminded him that he wanted her fired! I only stood up to Steve like that when I felt strongly enough about something (or someone) that I believed required it and, in this case, he realized that I was right.

There are several other examples of those who stood up to Steve, but the funniest one I can recall involved Eddy Cue.

Eddy was working in IT and was given the charter to propose an online store. He was a confident young man and came to the meeting very prepared to give his presentation. During his presentation Steve interrupted him, as he was known to do, and said confusingly, "Um, who are you?" He looked around the room, apparently for some answer, but everyone sat quietly. He turned back to Eddy, who was about to answer him, but Steve said, "Look, just sit down, you have no idea what you're talking about."

Reluctantly, Eddy did as he was told but people could tell by the look on his face that he really wanted to finish that presentation. Steve then got up and started talking about the same topic. At one point, as Steve was still talking, Eddy interrupted him to point out a positive thing that he had done that he felt Steve had skipped over. Everyone watched in disbelief. When Eddy, clearly nervous, was done talking Steve pointed at him and said, "I thought I told you to sit down and shut up." Eddy apologized and Steve went back to presenting.

Minutes later, Eddy interrupted him a second time with a quick clarification. Steve shot him an angry glare but did not dispute Eddy's point. Steve once again went back to presenting and, moments later, Eddy interrupted him yet *again*, this time to add what he believed to be a good idea. Steve was incredulous, but once again let him finish. When Eddy was done talking, we could tell he was clearly putting his resume together in his head. But this time, instead of Steve interrupting Eddy, he paused for several moments and said to Eddy, "You know what . . . you're right. That's a really good idea."

Eddy Cue is an example that if someone at Apple really knew what they were talking about and believed in it enough to fight for it, they would earn Steve's respect. Eddy would eventually go on to become Senior Vice President of Software and Services at Apple and one of the company's most powerful and influential leaders. The point is that visionaries like Steve often have a low tolerance for fools, but those who are able to earn their trust and respect will almost always get to stick around for the ride.

CHAPTER 14

THE STEVE I KNEW

*"Being the richest man in the cemetery doesn't
matter to me. Going to bed at night saying we've
done something wonderful, that's what matters to me."*

—STEVE JOBS

Beneath Steve's public persona as a visionary, there was another Steve, a more personal one who not a lot of people had the opportunity to know. It's this Steve that most of the biographies and movies have either failed to capture or, more often than not, got wrong. To those of us who knew him, most characterizations were exaggerated and sometimes just pure fiction. I'd have to agree with my friend, Steve Wozniak, who still tells anyone who asks, that the historical accuracy of most of those accounts are "pure, unadulterated bullshit!" Many of the popular portrayals have put a lot of focus on what they perceive to have been his negative aspects and make him out to have been a ruthless taskmaster. But as I've mentioned, that was certainly not the Steve I knew, and if I had to pick a single word to describe his personal side, it would be *complex*.

He could be your biggest supporter and simultaneously your biggest critic. There were times he would praise and fight for you publicly but excoriate you in private. But he was always firm in his approach and could easily justify his reasons for having such demanding expectations, explaining in an interview, "My job is not to be easy on people. My job is to make them better." His complexities came via a vast array of traits, behaviors and characteristics. He was passionate, creative, unconventional, purposeful, blunt, challenging, impatient, funny, thoughtful, appreciative, and yes, imperfect—all rolled into one. Everyone who existed in Steve's orbit knew him differently, and each of us have shared things about him that others never knew.

20 YEARS OF FRIENDSHIP

As I connect the dots throughout my professional life, the ones that overshadow all others were clearly my two stints at Apple. They were both life-changing, but as the saying goes, "Life isn't about what you experience, it's about who you experience it with." I was fortunate enough to have had the opportunity to experience mine with one of the greatest visionaries of all time. Even though he was Apple's leader, he always made it feel as though I was a peer and that he viewed me as a valuable asset to the company and to him personally. That has always meant a lot to me and is something I'll never forget.

Steve was an extraordinary leader and mentor, but I also considered him to be a good friend. However, it was never obvious if he saw anyone at Apple, including myself, as friends rather than just colleagues. We would often speak about non-business topics in a friendly manner, but I still wasn't sure that he actually considered me a *friend*—that is until we were both at a dinner in Paris celebrating the opening of the city's first retail Apple Store.

Dozens of Apple executives were scrambling around for a chance to sit by Steve during the event, or at least get his attention. I was sitting across the table in an exceptionally good mood, because I loved Paris and was still pumped about the opening ceremony. Then, much to my surprise, he picked up a glass of wine (something I had *never* seen him do), looked across at me and said, "John, here's to twenty years of friendship." I was never entirely sure why he said that at that specific moment. There was nothing particularly special going on between us that night that might have warranted such a nice remark, but it was sure nice to hear. It was also a moment I'll never forget, because I had rarely ever heard him publicly refer to *any* of his colleagues in such a way. He just didn't do things like that. He really *was* a complex person.

Another nice thing Steve said took place when my former wife, Tara, and I were attending a product introduction on the Apple campus in Cupertino. Ever since the introduction of Macintosh, Apple revealed new products in ways that were unforgettable. Steve always had a flair for extravagant marketing, and I was excited to bring Tara along with me for this one. As much as she'd heard me talk about him over the years, she had not actually met him at that point, so after the event ended, I walked her over to him and made the introduction. He was very gracious, and after sharing pleasantries, put his arm around my shoulder and said, "Tara, this is a good man." It was another touching moment that I didn't see coming and another small token of appreciation that meant a lot. Now I'm sure these comments may sound like throwaway lines to many people, but the truth was that these were the types of things Steve never really said.

TRUST ISSUES

There was one personal moment that happened between Steve and me that I feel sheds light on his complexity in ways that not many people understand. In 1982 we were traveling together in Europe and, while boarding a plane in Italy, the pilot suddenly announced there had been a bomb threat, and that we were to remain seated while they removed the luggage from the plane. We looked at each other confusedly, as neither of us had been in this type of situation before. The bomb threat was serious, we agreed, but the bigger question we had was "Why the hell are they removing our *luggage* from the plane? Shouldn't they be removing us?" It was quite an unnerving time for us both.

As we waited for what seemed like an eternity to deboard the plane, Steve turned to me and said, "You know John, I really admire you. You work as hard as I do and yet, you're happily married with a family. I'd like to get married and have a family too." It was rare for him to talk about such personal things. But the real kicker was what he asked me next. "Where do you think I could meet a good wife?"

I couldn't tell at first whether Steve was being serious or just making conversation to take our minds off the situation but realized that he was actually awaiting an answer. Up to that point I hadn't even realized such things crossed his mind, as he had always been obsessed with work and never really found time for much else, let alone a family! "Well, I don't know, Steve," I said. "I met my wife in college, but you didn't go to college. You might be able to meet someone in church, but you don't go to church." I reviewed a few other if/then scenarios before we finally came to the conclusion that it was hopeless. The main reason finding someone was so difficult, he believed, was because he could never tell if people were interested in him because of his notoriety and wealth or if they just really liked *him*.

After that conversation, I came to realize that a personal life had alluded him not because he didn't desire one but because it was just too difficult for him to trust people. It became abundantly clear that one of the biggest downsides to having enormous wealth or widespread celebrity status is loneliness.

Years later, when Steve knew the end was near, he called me and we had a nice long chat. The most memorable thing he said to me during that call was, "John, you are one of the most trustworthy people I know." Knowing that he had so many trust issues with people throughout his life, this meant a lot. Comments like these may seem trivial to some people, but those who knew Steve knew that compliments and expressing positive emotions were not his strong suit. Thus, whenever he did say things like this, no matter how small, it must have meant a lot to him, just as it did to me.

After Apple's IPO in late 1980, I remember how happy we all were that it was successful and that all those years of risks, sacrifices, and hard work had paid off. I would argue that one of the biggest IPO payoffs, for most of us at Apple, came in the form of validation that there really was a viable market for the personal computer. We always knew we were doing something special that *could* change the world, but we weren't so sure that the potential that we saw in them would also be recognized by the rest of the world. Both Steve and Apple had a lot of critics back then and many viewed us as little more than a wannabe startup trying to compete in an existing market with "big boys" like DEC, HP and IBM. But those of us on the inside knew better and our IPO's success was validation—especially for Steve.

One of the most interesting things about the IPO process was how differently people acted toward us. The media, and much of the public, seemed to care more about our newfound wealth than any of our products. Associates who had barely spoken to us before had now miraculously become our "best friends." Things were actually quite confusing for a while.

After my plane trip with Steve, I thought back to that confusing time and realized that he, being a public figure, must feel like that *all* the time. So, when he asked me how he could find a wife, what he was really asking was how to *trust*.

NEVER ABOUT MONEY

To some people becoming wealthy is their goal rather than a means to an end. But most of these people lack the vision, passion and persistence that's required to sustain the inevitable failings they'll face along the way. It's far more difficult to achieve meaningful success when one's focus is on a specific outcome (i.e. financial rewards) rather than on the process. Steve never cared about getting rich. In all the years I knew him I never once heard him bring up the importance of personal wealth. His focus was always on designing the best products he could and getting them into the hands of people he believed needed them. Ironically, I believe that focusing so little on money was one of the reasons he ended up with so much. Like the old saying goes, "If you take care of the top of the line, the bottom line takes care of itself."

I knew from the start that Steve wasn't in it for the money, but that fact really sunk in shortly after our IPO. We were both living in Los Gatos at the time and our houses were within walking distance of each other. His house was always impeccably maintained, but also a bit sparse when it came to furniture. In fact, he didn't have a lot in it at all other than a Maxfield Parrish painting, a Tiffany lamp, a Swedish stereo system, a mattress on the floor, and a three-drawer dresser. One day I was walking over to visit him and saw a piece of paper lying on his front lawn. This was unusual because he kept his house as clean as his yard. I picked up the paper to throw in the trash, but when I saw what it actually was, I was stunned. This piece of "trash" was actually an Apple stock certificate for 7.5 million shares, at the time worth around $400 million. I knocked on Steve's door and when he opened it I handed him the certificate and said, "I believe this belongs to you." He glanced at it, laughed and said, "Thanks, I guess it must have blown out the window or something." He then casually opened the dresser and tossed it in the top drawer.

That's when I realized that he *really* didn't care about the money. Years later, during an interview he was giving on education, I heard a reporter ask him specifically about his wealth. Steve just brushed off the question with a clever quip about how money is just used by people as a "yardstick" and then, in the same breath, shifted the conversation back to something he actually cared about—students. "The neatest thing was, by 1979, I was able to walk into classrooms that had 15 Apple computers and see the kids using them," he said. "*Those* are the kinds of things that are really the milestones." That was the Steve I knew.

Thirty-one years after I had found that stock certificate lying in Steve's yard, I was invited to his memorial service at the Stanford chapel. In attendance was Larry Ellison, the co-founder of Oracle, and one of Steve's close businesses associates. Larry is someone so wealthy that he makes other billionaires feel poor by comparison. At the time, according to *Forbes* magazine, he was the fifth richest person in the world with a reported net worth of $40 billion and, as of July 2020, he was instead worth a little over $72 billion.

Larry had been an Apple board member and Steve's friend for years, so it wasn't a surprise to see him at the memorial service, wanting to say a few words about the Steve *he* knew. One of the stories he shared that day reminded me a lot of that lost stock certificate. He talked about how he and Steve both owned homes in Hawaii and how one day they were walking along the beach discussing whether or not Steve should return to Apple. Larry told him that with their combined net worth they could do a takeover of Apple and make a ton of money. He said that Steve then stopped walking, looked at him and said, "Larry, we don't need any more money. I need to do it because it's the right thing to do." Not surprisingly, Steve had felt the same way about money at 55 years old as he did at 25.

QUIET PHILANTHROPY

Upon Bill Gates' retirement from Microsoft, he became a full-time philanthropist by starting the Bill and Melinda Gates Foundation. Today he deservedly gets as much credit and public recognition for the good his foundation does as he does for founding and running Microsoft. Conversely, Steve rarely ever got public attention for his charitable giving, and in some cases he even got *negative* attention for supposedly not giving enough! Even today, many people don't realize that Steve was actually an active philanthropist who gave away millions to causes he cared about, which included donations to nonprofits, charitable events, individuals in need of help, and R&D for serious diseases like cancer and AIDS.

The main reason most people don't know much about his charitable giving is because he didn't want them to. While Bill Gates is a public philanthropist, Steve Jobs was a private one who preferred quiet, anonymous giving. Many wealthy people and companies give to causes and organizations and they also happily accept the benefits that come from doing so. Things like public praise, goodwill, brand image, and brand awareness are common examples, but so are more tangible things such as tax write-offs, board seats, and even entire buildings named after them. Indeed, there are a lot of benefits to being a public philanthropist, but Steve never felt as though he needed public acceptance.

I have nothing against public philanthropy and have given quite a bit away publicly myself. I feel like the more we can do to help the better, but I also think it's important to at least recognize the difference between public philanthropy and what I call "quiet philanthropy." Steve may have sometimes been loud in Apple executive meetings, but when it came to philanthropy, he almost always preferred silence. What most people don't know is that nearly all of his donations were given anonymously with explicit instructions that they remain that way. As public as his life was, and continues to be, the Steve I knew was actually a private person who more often than not preferred to keep it that way.

Even though the majority of his donations were given anonymously, there were a few times when it was either leaked that he was a donor, or that a large donation was given through Apple with his blessings. When donations are given through public companies, the company is required to share this information as part of their financial disclosures. One of Steve's few high-profile public philanthropy examples happened this way. In 2006, Apple partnered with Bono, the lead singer of the band U2, to raise money for the musician's Product Red AIDS Fund. Apple created a line of red iPods and accessories for iPods, iPads, and iPhones meant to bring attention to the cause. Ten percent of every Product Red item that sold went to Bono's AIDS charity.

But even as this was happening, there continued to be media coverage critical of the lack of public charitable giving by Steve and Apple. In response, Bono stood up for him publicly, even going so far as to write a letter to *The New York Times* saying that Steve, via Apple, was by far the largest benefactor to the Global Fund to Fight AIDS, Tuberculosis and Malaria, with contributions numbering in the tens of millions. Bono went on to say that when he approached Steve about the possibility of partnering, Steve agreed without hesitation, specifically telling him, "There is nothing better than the chance to save lives." This drive to save lives also led him to successfully lobby California lawmakers to make the state the first in the country to create a live donor registry for kidney transplants, a move that other states would soon follow.

MAKING A DIFFERENCE

Steve and Apple also made a difference in the lives of individuals. For example, it never ceases to amaze me how much influence a well-designed product can have on people. In 2004, a fifth-grade boy sent Steve a letter, handwritten on wide-ruled paper, in which he talked about how he was frustrated because his school did not have Apple computers. He argued in the letter that Macs were much better than the PCs at his school, because they would allow him to more easily do the kinds of creative projects he had wanted to do. He briefly explained what those projects were and concluded his letter by asking Steve if he'd be willing to send him a Mac.

I suspect that when Steve read this letter it may have reminded him of his own early days reaching out to Bill Hewlett at HP, asking him for those spare computer parts. At Apple we received hundreds of inquiries every day asking for one thing or another, but this particular letter stood out, because it was genuine, personal, and touched on a lot of things that Steve and I had been talking about. He gave the letter to me and, after I read it, I was impressed and really respected the honesty and initiative.

I sent the kid a free Macintosh in the hopes that it would help him achieve his goals. Years went by and I had forgotten all about the gift, but the kid had not forgotten about Apple. During his senior year of high school, he sent me a copy of his admission essay to Stanford University. He wrote that because I had sent him that Macintosh, I was one of three people in the world who had made the biggest difference in his life. He talked about how he was able to use that Mac to choreograph school plays, design projects, and perform a number of creative endeavors that led in his ultimate success. Several months later I heard from the young man again, this time informing me that he had been accepted into Stanford's computer science program and wanted to know if we could have lunch so he could meet me in person. This is just one example of the thousands of gifts Steve, and others at Apple, provided that had such an incredible impact on individual lives without getting or needing media publicity.

I also view that story as an example of Steve's constant belief that the power of products can make a tremendous difference in people's lives. He truly believed in the power of Apple products and that, so long as we got them right, they would always be the best way to give back. He once explained to me that his real gift to society was creating cutting-edge platforms on which people could create software, programs, and apps, especially ones that could give organizations the ability to bring in even more giving. One of my biggest takeaways from being with Steve was that money is fleeting and once it's gone, it's gone. What *would* make the biggest difference in the world, he taught me, were well-designed platforms and ecosystems. He felt that by creating digital platforms with active ecosystems, we would be able to give charitable organizations the means to raise far more money than any single individual or company ever could. I have come to think of this as the twenty-first- century version of the classic maxim, "Give a man a fish and you feed him for a day, teach him to fish and you feed him for life." The Steve I knew handed out plenty of fish but was far more determined to be the one creating and delivering the best fishing poles the world had ever seen.

CHAPTER 15

STEVE'S LEGACY

"I'm a long-term kind of person."

—STEVE JOBS

I first learned about Steve's pancreatic cancer in the summer of 2004 along with the rest of Apple's employees. Only Steve's family and doctors had known of his earlier diagnosis, so it caught everyone off-guard to hear such a startling announcement. I, for one, hadn't noticed any physical signs of his sickness, but knew the prognosis for this disease was poor and felt distraught at the thought of losing him. He was just 56 years old and now I feared that he may have been right all along about his fear of dying young. I was eight years older than him, so hearing such tragic news was also a big wake-up call for me and a humbling reminder that tomorrow is never guaranteed and that every day is a gift to be cherished.

I learned later that Steve had rebuffed traditional medical treatments, which were meant to control the cancer, in favor of simply altering his diet and experimenting with different types of alternative medicine. When he realized it wasn't working, he decided to have surgery, admitting that he should not have focused exclusively on the use of alternative medicine.

When it was announced that he would be taking an immediate leave of absence, Tim Cook took control of Apple as interim-CEO. Shortly after Steve's leaving, it was announced that his surgery was successful, that he was now cancer-free, and now he was just taking time to recover. I really wanted to believe that he had been cured but remember feeling cautiously relieved at hearing the news. I felt much better when I saw Steve return to Apple in good spirits and jumping back into his work right where he had left off. Unfortunately, things would not remain that way for very long.

Between 2006 and 2008 Steve began looking frail and I knew something wasn't right. While his mind was still quite active, his body was suffering, and I had the terrifying feeling that the cancer had returned. In August of 2008 *Bloomberg News* erroneously published Steve's obituary, in spite of the fact that he was sitting in our Wednesday morning executive meeting when the "news" broke! Steve found it hilarious and commented on the blunder at his next keynote speech, saying, "Reports of my death are greatly exaggerated." His sense of humor was a beacon of light in a dark situation.

It wasn't until December of 2008 when Phil Schiller presented a keynote address that Steve would normally give, that we knew something was really wrong. Our fears were realized when, in April of that year, we got a memo saying that Steve's health was "more complicated" than he had thought and that he would be taking a second leave of absence. He was placing Tim back in charge as CEO, he said, while he would be taking on the role of chairman of the board. This time, while he was away, he underwent a successful liver transplant and then returned to Apple again as CEO in 2009. But come January of 2011 we learned he would be taking a third leave of absence and in August of that year he resigned as Apple's CEO. Then, on October 5, 2011, Steve Jobs, my boss, mentor, and friend, passed away in his home while surrounded by family. His last words were said to be, "Oh wow. Oh wow. Oh wow."

HEARING THE NEWS

When I heard the news of Steve's death I was in a car in Texas with Bill Rankin, a member of my education team, on the way to give a presentation. I had painfully watched him deteriorate physically over the last couple of years and knew this day was coming. Still, hearing it put a huge burden on my heart. While I still ended up honoring my commitment to give that presentation in Texas, it was the most difficult one I have ever given.

I will always admire how well Steve was able to handle the entire situation prior to his death. I never saw or heard him complain or blame anything or anyone. I just saw him continue working hard over long hours and remaining positive and passionate. I wasn't at all surprised when Tim Cook said his last conversation with Steve was not about anything personal but that it was all work-related. Right up to the very end he remained dedicated to his vision and to ensuring that Apple was in the best position possible to bring it to life.

I sometimes ask myself *if I were to find out that I only had a year left to live, what would I spend it doing?* Most likely I would be getting all of my affairs in order and rushing to check things off my bucket list. But Steve was just so committed to realizing his vision that he worked tirelessly until the very end. Not even a deadly disease could stop him from pushing forward, which I couldn't help but respect. The last thing Steve supposedly penned before he died was something that I continue to find powerful and profound: "You can hire someone to drive your car, but you can't hire them to lay in your sick bed."

LOOKING BACK

In my mind Steve wasn't just Apple's founder, he *was* Apple. He changed the world, and on a more personal level, he changed my life and the lives of my family for generations to come. Whether directly or indirectly, he has impacted the lives of millions of Apple shareholders, businesses, and customers, as well as their families, both present and future. It's hard to believe that one person could have such a tremendous impact on so many others in so many ways. I am truly blessed and honored that Steve personally chose me to be a part of his world and work by his side not once, but twice!

It was also memorable to be in the rare position to have witnessed firsthand his growth over the years, both as a leader and a person. I watched him grow from a naïve young man with a dream, into a visionary who stopped at nothing to reach his goals. I watched as he grew from an inexperienced manager to a mature, experienced and powerful leader. I watched as he grew from a man who avoided failure, to one who embraced it and used it as inspiration. I watched as he grew from an insensitive man who couldn't understand or tolerate ideas and beliefs that didn't match his own, to the man who would later tell me that he respected my religious beliefs.

I also found Steve to be extremely well read and was impressed by his keen understanding of history. When he talked about the personal computer, he would often equate it to the motor and describe how it began life as a humungous contraption with little practical, day-to-day use, until evolving into microsized machines that existed in every household around the world, powering everything from watches to toys. But the Steve I knew was always more interested in empowering people than instruments, which is why he focused so intently on providing the best experience for individual end users, even if it meant passing up lucrative opportunities to sell more broadly to corporations.

Steve taught me how to always follow my instincts, trust myself, and think differently rather than blindly following others, wisdom that I believe was best captured by his Stanford commencement speech. My biggest takeaway from that speech was to take the time to look back, understand, and connect the dots of the past in ways that will inform and guide new, meaningful dots in the future.

Steve's legacy is now secure. His name will forever be synonymous with the greatest of business leaders, and his visionary leadership will continue to inspire new generations of artists, inventors, and entrepreneurs around the world. He has directly changed, or heavily influenced, dozens of industries ranging from computer hardware and software, to mobile devices, music, telephones, televisions, cameras, calculators, stocks, and the way we access the internet. After all this, it's ironic that he would also say, "I'm actually as proud of many of the things we haven't done as the things we have done."

I was recently asked what I would say if I could go back and have one last conversation with Steve before he died. I didn't have an answer at the time, but after thinking about it more, I've come to the conclusion that I would first admit to him that I should have pushed harder to let him lead Lisa's team, while I handled the management responsibilities. I had always felt that way, but never got the chance to tell him. Next, I would share more of my faith with him, not to try and convert him, but to reassure him that many of us believe there is an afterlife and that even though he may be leaving, he will never really be gone. His memory, his incredible spirit, and his legacy will continue to live forever. Whether he would have agreed with me on any of this or not is a different story, but I think he would have listened and not written it off as impossible, because he didn't believe anything was impossible.

ONE MORE STEVE

At the end of most of Apple's product introduction events, Steve, ever the showman, would use one of his more endearing phrases, "Oh yeah, there's one more thing." The famous line, now referred to as the "one more thing," became so common that employees and media alike had come to eagerly expect it. What he meant by it was that he had been saving something important that he wanted to share, whether it was a new product, a key announcement, a special music performance, etc. With that in mind I now present my own *one more thing*: Woz.

As much as I admired and respected Steve Jobs right from the start, he was not the only Steve I felt that way about at Apple. From the moment I started working there, a seed had been planted that would eventually grow into a meaningful and important relationship with another company co-founder, Steve "Woz" Wozniak—the *other* Steve I know. Even before joining the company, I knew exactly who he was, although I had not yet had the pleasure of meeting him personally. Well before my arrival he had already earned a reputation among Silicon Valley engineers for developing the Apple I. While Jobs was not that well-known yet, Woz, from a technical standpoint, was considered by many in the industry to be an engineering guru.

Woz was pretty quiet and often kept to himself, buried in the schematics of one of the many projects he was always working on. He never had any real interest in running the business side of Apple, preferring instead to focus on designing and building the products that made the company possible. Over the years, as the two of us got to know each other better, we realized that we had a lot in common. We were both Berkeley graduates, engineering wonks, and former Hewlett-Packard employees. We both had a passion for education and a love for Top Dog, a local Berkeley hot dog stand (and possibly the best brand of hot dogs on the West Coast!). We were also both extremely fascinated with computers, software for me, hardware for him. Our commonalities and corresponding conversations would ultimately lead to a long-lasting friendship that continues today.

POLAR OPPOSITES

While Woz and I did have a lot in common, he and his fellow Apple co-founder, Steve Jobs, did not. They had been friends for years prior to founding the company, but that friendship was based more on the theory that opposites attract than on any shared interests. They did both love the *potential* of technology, but in very different ways. Jobs was highly ambitious, wanting Apple to build products that would change the world. Comparatively, Woz was quite unambitious, except when it came to building computers and gadgets. He never wanted to build revolutionary products to change the world, he wanted to build them to see if he could.

One could easily make the argument that Jobs and Woz were polar opposites, and for the most part they'd be right, but this also made the two a perfect match. The way I like to think of it is that Jobs was the brain behind Apple and Woz was its heart. Jobs was a marketing genius, but not a great engineer, whereas Woz was a legendary engineer, but could care less about marketing. As passionate and ambitious as Jobs was about turning Apple into the greatest company in the world, Woz was just as passionate about making his inventions the best in the world. Neither of them ever cared much for money in and of itself. Jobs cared about it only so much as it allowed him to continue doing what he needed to realize his vision and Woz cared about it only so much as it would continue funding his ability to build better machines.

I knew Steve Jobs was a nice person, but he didn't often reveal that side of himself publicly. Woz, on the other hand, is probably the kindest person I have ever met, and has never had any qualms with people knowing this about him. It may be partially due to Woz's kindness that Jobs was sometimes perceived as being so harsh. But that wasn't fair because, compared to Woz, *most* of us might come across that way! You could say that Woz on one end of the spectrum and Jobs on the other in a Silicon Valley were a rendition of the classic good cop, bad cop.

Woz was known around Apple for how nice he was even more so than he was for his infamous pranks. In those early years there were two acts of his that really stood out. The first happened prior to my arriving at Apple when, not long after he had finished building the Apple I, he decided to freely give away its design. He essentially had an "open-source" mentality before the phrase was even used—like Jobs, Woz was ahead of his time. All Woz ever really wanted to do with his multitude of inventions was share them in ways that would help others.

Another Woz moment that stood out happened just after Apple's initial public offering, when he had suddenly found himself worth hundreds of millions of dollars. The first two things that most Apple employees with stock options did after the IPO was invest their money and buy a home. In contrast, Woz's first inclination after the IPO wasn't to spend or invest the money, but to give it right back. He set up a table in Apple's cafeteria and proceeded to transfer a number of his personal shares of Apple stock, at a *substantially* reduced, pre-IPO, price, to the Apple employees who had not been awarded stock options. It was an incredibly unselfish thing to do, but Woz didn't think much of it because it just seemed like the obvious thing to do. Watching him do that was amazing and it would ultimately become a major influence on my own charitable giving.

EXTENDED FAMILY

While Woz and I were friendly throughout Apple's earliest years, it wasn't until after his plane crash in 1981 that we really became close. When I heard the news, I canceled my weekend getaway and drove quickly to the hospital to be with him and his family. Sitting in that hospital lobby not knowing if he was going to make it or not was one of the scariest moments of my life. I prayed a lot during that time and thanked God when I learned that he would live.

Another thing that brought Woz and me closer came not long after my return to Apple. Having worked at a school for the previous decade, I had come back with a deep appreciation and passion for education. By this point he had pretty much completely separated himself from Apple and, apart from working on a new remote-control device that he'd come up with, he was heavily focused on giving computers to kids in public schools and, just as importantly, taking the time to visit classrooms and teach the kids how to use them. It was this shared love of education that really helped to bond our friendship. Without my asking, Woz even provided me with free workspace in his office complex which ended up giving us even *more* time to bond.

During that time, I came to realize just how much Woz loved children, which is why he got so involved in education. He had a very youthful spirit, always preferring to hang out with fun kids over boring adults. Wherever he went he took along his infamous bag of tricks that consisted of a variety of math puzzles and critical-thinking games. He also has a deep love of playing video games, being particularly fond of the classic tile-matching game Tetris. Woz was so into Tetris that he's (still) known to sit in the very back at events and concerts so that he can play it on his Game Boy without anyone noticing!

But I'd say the thing that really sealed the deal with our friendship was when he fell in love with Janet Hill, a colleague who worked with me and someone who I considered to be a very close friend. I first met Janet around 1998 at the NECC conference where she had been given the task of giving Apple T-shirts to those of us working our booth. She had no idea who I was, that I was one of Apple's earliest employees, or that I was currently a Vice President. When I approached her table to get my shirt I smiled and said, "Hi, I'm John Couch. Do you mind if I get an extra shirt for a special friend?"

Janet smiled and promptly asked for my Apple ID badge. As I began checking my pockets to see if I had even brought it, the young lady working beside Janet leaned over and whispered to her that I was the new Vice President of Education *and* her boss. Janet looked incredibly embarrassed and, just as I found my badge and began to show it to her, she was already insisting that I could "take as many T-shirts" as I wanted. Soon after that we began working together and would continue doing so for the next fifteen years.

Many years after that incident, Janet confessed that she thought that I was going to fire her that day, but that thought had never even crossed my mind. I actually found the whole episode endearing. Oh, and that "special friend" of mine? She eventually became my wife, which I guess shows the power of an Apple T-shirt!

Because Janet was such a sweet and caring person, it came as no surprise when I learned that she and Woz had met on a "geek" cruise and fallen in love. In 2008 they tied the knot, but Woz being Woz, a traditional wedding was out of the question. So, instead of getting married in a church like most couples, they decided to get hitched at a Segway conference! Instead of walking down the aisle, this bride and groom came *zooming* down it on motorized Segways.

Of course, now that Janet was being christened Janet *Wozniak*, she could have easily just retired to great wealth, but instead chose to stick around and work because she believed so much in what we were doing at Apple Education.

The Wozniaks continue to be two of the nicest people I know, and we have now become what amounts to an extended family. They are frequent guests at my home for dinner and wine and, in early 2021, my winery, Eden Estate Wines, even released a special-edition vintage named "Woz's Chardonnay," in honor of our decades-long friendship.

CHAPTER 16

A DIFFERENT APPLE

*"I didn't see it then, but it turned out that getting
fired from Apple was the best thing that could
have ever happened to me."*

—STEVE JOBS

I was fortunate to have been able to spend over sixteen years as a champion of Apple's education business. I feel as though I learned as much in my role as VP of Education as the teachers and students I spent my time trying to help. When Steve oversaw Apple, whether as VP of New Products, chairman, or CEO, he established a culture that was unlike any other company. It was designed around rapid growth and relied heavily on creativity, crazy ideas, risk-taking, and a single shared vision across the company. He was never afraid of breaking rules or ignoring established organizational hierarchies and norms, and he almost always chose innovation, intuition, and instinct over traditional routes. This is what made it feel so special to work at Apple.

But even the best things eventually come to an end, and after Steve's death it started to feel like it may have been the beginning of the end of the Apple I had grown to love. Making matters worse, my trusted Sales Animal, Barry Wright, had announced his retirement, which I knew was going to be a devastating blow to Apple and particularly to our education division. Barry and I had become quite close over 10 years and even though he may have officially reported to me, he truly was my equal. He was a crucial member of the education team and, as head of sales, one of the main reasons we were able to grow the business to $9.1 billion in just years. In fact, Barry had become such an influential figure at Apple, and a trusted ally of mine, that I encouraged him to work directly with CEO Tim Cook on *all* sales issues. I believed doing this was one of my best decisions, because it allowed the entire company to benefit from Barry's incredible talents rather than limited them to education. Of course, that also meant that his retirement would be a huge blow to Apple as a whole, rather than to just my division. Now, with our visionary leader and our incredibly effective sales animal both gone, I knew Apple would not be the same. I also expected that changes were coming to the education division, but what I didn't anticipate was that I would now be working at an *entirely* different Apple.

TIM'S APPLE

After Steve's death, Tim Cook became CEO of Apple and immediately took on a tremendous amount of new responsibility. Shortly after Barry retired, Tim began implementing major changes throughout the company, which included a significant change in the organization of the education division. Recall that after Steve brought me back to Apple, he tasked me with fixing our declining education business, but confessed that he wasn't sure whether the bigger problem was sales or marketing. In an effort to improve both, he directed that the education division be organized differently. Rather than being organized by function, like other Apple divisions, he wanted education to be more cohesive, with marketing and sales functions to operate under a single vice president—by which he meant me. This allowed me to not have to worry about communication issues across sales and marketing, because instead of overseeing one or the other, I was in the fortunate, albeit unique, position of managing both and the gamble paid off. But now Tim Cook was in charge and he had other ideas.

While Steve was still in charge, my education division as a whole reported to Tim. But now that he was gone, Tim decided to revert back to a functional organization, so that education would be more in line with Apple's traditional organizational structure. To accomplish this, he decided to remove Education's entire sales team from my purview and have them instead report to Apple's new Vice President of Sales, a former CFO at United Airlines. He would then, in turn, hire his own *sales*-based Vice President of Education, meaning that not only was the education division split in half, there were also now two VPs of Education!

I was not crazy about this change, because it meant that Apple Education, a unique division that knew exactly how to serve our customers, was now going to become much more generalized and be run by individuals who may have known sales in general but did not necessarily understand the intricacies of the education market. This change went completely against Steve's vision for rebuilding Apple Education, in which we believed the focus needed to be on building student and teacher learning environments rather than just selling boxes. But Tim was now in charge and the decision was made to tear down Apple's education division and rebuild it the way it was during its decade-long stretch of declining sales.

The changes to Apple Education did not stop there. Now that education sales had been separated, it was now overseen by a VP of Education Sales (the first of *four* by the time I retired!). Tim also decided that the marketing team and I should be moved and that the most logical place for us was in product marketing, which was overseen by Apple's VP of Product

Marketing, Phil Schiller. Literally overnight, I was now part of the marketing team and would be reporting to an entirely new boss.

The one silver lining was that I already knew and liked Phil, having attended his weekly management meetings. For years Phil had overseen all of Apple's product marketing activities—that is, except for education. Phil's role in educational marketing had, until now, been mainly limited to giving final approval of our larger proposed marketing programs and using his influence to help move things along. Now he would be adding to his already full plate, the responsibility of education marketing, which I knew was a lot. I was still VP of Education, only now I was officially a part of Apple's product marketing group with no sales responsibility.

Phil and I had different management styles, but I always had a tremendous amount of respect for him. My biggest concern at this point though had to do with the complex intricacies of the education marketplace. These were not things that could be easily explained, much less quickly understood. In the United States, for instance, there is no single "education market," there are thousands. There are different laws, policies, and guidelines in every state, county, city, district, and even individual schools. Trying to position and sell technology in education could not be successfully done through one-size-fits-all messaging like most other consumer products.

To Phil's credit, he did take the time to listen to my concerns and clearly recognized the difficulties and challenges within the education market. He was extremely supportive of the direction I wanted to go with education, which he understood was an extension of Steve's vision. Phil even told me, "You probably forgot more about education than I know," which was quite a compliment, especially considering that prior to that I made the biggest faux pas by referring to his alma mater, Boston College, as Boston University!

GOVERNMENT AFFAIRS

I had been working with Phil for several years on his product marketing team when suddenly a new opportunity presented itself. Tim Cook was looking to clarify Apple's values and, to communicate this, he applied his own version of an analogy that had been used by Steve years earlier. Steve had described Apple's core businesses as being equivalent to the three legs of a stool, which he said consisted of Macintosh, iPhones, and iTunes. As with all of Steve's analogies this helped simplify things and kept the entire Apple team focused on shared goals and the big picture. Tim was now redefining Apple's cultural focus as a *four*-legged stool that included: Diversity, Privacy and Security, Environment and...*Education*.

I was encouraged and optimistic because our CEO was now *officially* listing education as one of Apple's "core values," coming closer to aligning with Steve's idea of education being in "Apple's DNA." I assumed that Tim's new declaration meant Apple would now be placing a much greater emphasis on education, and use that as a starting point for designing, building, and selling innovative tools that would improve it. Unfortunately, it didn't turn out that way. Instead, I was moved out of product marketing and sent to work for Lisa Jackson, Executive Vice President of Apple's Government and Community Affairs.

I was hopeful that by working in this new area I would be able get a lot done in terms of creating or restructuring education programs. Tim had made a pledge that Apple would donate $100 million to the federal government's ConnectEd program, an ambitious initiative that aimed to bring reliable, high-speed broadband to every school across the United States. Apple's pledge meant that hundreds of low-income schools would have access to key learning resources such as iPads and

MacBooks. It also meant that for the first time Apple had close ties with the federal government, which I knew could lead to various new opportunities. Lisa's Government and Community Affairs team had recently inherited Apple's involvement in ConnectED, which I had helped define as Apple's representative on President Obama's ConnectED task force.

One key thing I did while on this task force was make the decision that, rather than us asking people to submit open requests for proposals and turning down 99 percent of them, we would only invite proposals from those schools that had at least 96 percent of their students receiving free and reduced lunches. This not only limited the number of schools that could submit proposals, but also ensured that those who did were the ones that needed the most help.

After my arrival in the Government Affairs division, I explained to Lisa that the program was designed toward schools' strategical and tactical plans, teacher training, as well as upgrading their infrastructure and computers. The last thing I wanted to do, I told her, was dump technology onto schools when they had no idea how to use it. If there's one thing I knew about technology in education, it was that selling a bunch of computers to schools without effective teacher training hurts us long-term far more than it helps us short-term. Not only would doing this risk giving Apple a reputation for selling useless products, but it would also negatively impact the perception of *all* educational technology. Lisa was a good person, but single-handedly overseeing Apple's entire Government and Community Affairs Department was no small task. She was busy enough before I arrived but now, with ConnectEd dropped in her lap, her load was becoming overwhelming. So, it came as no surprise to me that she seemed less than enthusiastic about my education proposals and crazy ideas.

CRAZY IDEAS

As I began settling into my latest division, I continued to argue that teacher professional development needed to be a required part of any Apple educational donations. After months of intensive research, and backed up by irrefutable data, I presented my case to Lisa. I suggested that we make professional development free for any school that was an Apple 1 to 1 (one computer per student) partner, so that we were present at the school side by side with them for three to five years. Or more simply, I said, we could just treat all Apple 1 to 1 schools the same way as the ConnectEd schools.

A second idea that I knew would be beneficial and help ensure that education remained a core Apple value, was to make our education business a separate nonprofit. This would allow the nonprofit to focus on the "why," while supporting our for-profit sales and marketing teams. Plus, due to our new alliance with the federal government, operating through a nonprofit would distance us from the perceived profit motive and significantly improve our chances of gaining political support. It would also greatly expand the awareness and acceptance of our ACOT findings and of the challenge-based learning model inspired by those findings.

This could even be done, I said, without it costing much of anything. My justification for this was a study I did by totaling all the "gifts" handed out by every Apple department. The amount totaled one billion dollars, and yet no one at Apple had even realized that we were making that size of a contribution. If the profit from our education business was even 10 percent of sales, I noted, we could purposefully shift our previous piecemeal giving to education, which would have a huge impact. I was incredibly pumped that I might have been able to realize a couple of my crazy ideas, but they ultimately never made it past Lisa. It was disheartening that Apple now seemed content with maintaining the status quo, the very thing Steve had abhorred.

It didn't take long for Lisa to come to the realization that trying to take on my ambitious education ideas, on top of her primary responsibilities, was too much. One day I was called into her office where she explained the situation and recommended that I might have more success if I went to work for Susan Prescott, Apple's Enterprise and Education Product Manager, who in turn, worked for Phil Schiller in product marketing! I couldn't help but laugh, gently reminding her that I had already worked *directly* for Phil in marketing and asked why she thought my going back to work for someone who *reported* to Phil was such a good idea. She didn't have an answer. Walking out of her office that day, I couldn't help but think that Apple's four-legged stool might come crashing down, because its education leg was clearly breaking.

Despite my reservations, I did give the move some thought, but ultimately decided that going back to marketing made no sense. When I explained the situation to HR, I was relieved that they agreed. They also agreed with me that Lisa would likely never have time to dedicate to education, so keeping me there wasn't a good fit either. Instead, they proposed that, since all of the statewide conference and speaking engagements I was doing had opened major doors for education sales, perhaps I would consider a move to sales, where I could continue speaking as the "the face and voice for Apple Education." This *sounded* worthwhile, but it would also mean that I'd no longer have any operational responsibilities. It was a tough pill to swallow, but at that point I figured maybe it wasn't such a bad idea. Besides, I had gone from managing 750 people to none in just two short years, so what was the point of having operational responsibilities when there was no operation?

MUSICAL CHAIRS

Once again, I was on the move, this time joining the Apple sales department, where I would be working with Doug Beck, our VP of Worldwide Education Sales, who had just recently hired his own VP of U.S. Education Sales. From that point forward I would no longer have day to day managerial responsibilities at Apple, nor any direct involvement in educational sales or marketing, the very areas Steve had brought me back to oversee. But, as always, I decided to throw myself into my work and make the most of the opportunity. I began by increasing my speaking engagements, especially to state education boards and at superintendent conferences. I had always been passionate about the learning process, but it increased significantly in my new role, as I was now constantly meeting face to face with thousands of people who were directly on the frontlines of education. I also found my overt passion to be contagious, which intensified it even more!

It turned out that not only were my talks leading to an increase in Apple's overall educational sales, but they also had the added benefit of informing people about the overall potential of ed-tech throughout the learning process. I realized pretty early on that I had made the right decision in taking on this new role, because it was clearly a win-win-win scenario for Apple, teachers, and myself. Our ACOT² findings, CBL pedagogy, ConnectEd, Brazil Project, and other key projects (i.e., Knotion, Oxford Day Academy, Varmond, and more), were fueling a level of optimism for me that I hadn't had since Steve's passing. I finally had effective solutions for solving educational problems that had persisted for decades. But no matter how well my talks went, my message and ideas were still not reaching the number of people I needed to in order to bring those solutions to life. So, in my own time and at my own expense, I began working with Harvard University's Graduate School of Education to help redefine and simplify my message in ways that would reach a wider audience. The outcome of this alliance led to the writing of a book based on my talks: *Rewiring Education*.

REWIRING EDUCATION

Fixing education in America is no small task, and neither is writing a book on how to do it. I partnered up with Jason Towne, a graduate student at Harvard's Graduate School of Education, whose area of focus was education psychology, an important yet often ignored part of teaching and learning. With Jason's expertise on student motivation and my knowledge of education technology, I knew that together (with a combined 50 years of experience) we would be able to write a book like no other. It took us just over a year to write it, but once it was done, I knew it had effectively simplified my education presentations and, more importantly, perfectly captured Steve's (and our) vision for the future of education.

Rewiring Education presented a bold vision for education. It took an in-depth look at the role that motivational psychology plays in education and its direct relationship to the success (or failure) of education technology. It discussed our ability to recognize the nature of the digital native, looked at several new and emerging technologies (a lot of which Apple had already created), and explored ways that Apple's CBL research could become the basis for creating extraordinary learning environments that are relevant, creative, collaborative, and challenging. In other words, it was *exactly* the kind of book Apple needed to help spread its message.

FINAL DAYS

Two years prior to writing even a single word of the book, I had wanted to make sure I wasn't breaking any rules and that the Apple higher-ups knew it wasn't going to say anything negative about the company. To that end, I went over the book's purpose and content with Apple execs and lawyers and I even explained how Apple would indirectly benefit from it. I showed them that it was essentially just a more detailed version of the presentation I was already giving. It wasn't about Apple products, I told them, but it did show the importance ed tech to twenty-first-century learning, which would certainly help sell some of our more relevant products. "In fact," I noted, "it would be pretty clear to anyone reading it that the best partner for changing education was Apple, the company that's been by their side for over thirty years." I was thrilled when they gave me the green light to proceed.

Jason and I secured a contract with a well-established publisher and I found myself one step closer to realizing Steve's grand vision for education on a much larger scale. But alas, exactly one week prior to publication, I was summoned into Doug Beck's office and informed that Legal did "not want to set a precedent of Apple executives writing books"—even if the book wasn't about Apple! Had the date been April 1st I would have thought this was an April Fool's Day joke, but it wasn't, and he was being serious. I reminded him that he, Legal, and Apple leadership had known about this book for over a year and never said, or even implied, that I shouldn't write it. I also reminded him that a book on ACOT had already been published, so the precedent had already been set.

Doug shrugged and apologized but said there was nothing he could do about it. He then explained that I'd still be able to publish my book *if* I was willing to convert my role as VP of

Education into that of an independent contractor. In that capacity, he said, I could continue to speak for Apple Education
for one year, while still collecting my current salary. After that
year, they would begin reducing the number of talks and I'd
be paid on a talk-by-talk basis at a minimal rate. I wasn't crazy
about the idea of no longer being an Apple employee. I also
felt a bit betrayed considering they had known about this for
so long and said nothing. Now, after I was already bound by a
publishing contract, they all of a sudden had a problem with it.

On top of that, the way this "option" was presented made
it clear that it wasn't much of a choice at all. I was not crazy
about this. Nonetheless, I've learned over the years that the
higher we go up in age, the lower our patience level drops and,
at 72 years old, this wasn't really a fight I wanted to take on. I
was also tired of the musical chairs Apple had me playing the
past few years and was rapidly losing hope that any of my crazy
ideas to change education would ever be approved. Given that
I was nearing retirement anyway, I felt it was time to move
on. I would spread the rewiring education message myself and
find ways to realize Steve's vision for education without their
support. So, I agreed to their proposal, negotiated a severance
package and the details of my new role and just like that, for
the second time in my professional life, I was no longer an
Apple employee. Ironically, a year after my book's publication,
Apple CEO Tim Cook successfully published his own book.

AN EXTRAORDINARY RIDE

I honestly had mixed feelings about leaving Apple. On
one hand I was disappointed by the way my departure was handled and felt as though I was being forced to leave behind one
of the most important things in my life. On the other hand, I
was relieved that I was now free to focus on all aspects of education rather than just on sales. Sure, I would no longer be able

to use my influential title of "Vice President of Education," but before long I realized I never really needed to rely on it in the first place. I had always been more than just my title.

Not long after I left, Apple's share of the education market began to decline. As I warned, it was a mistake to focus on selling expensive boxes in the education market, rather than selling computers and tablets specifically *designed* to address teaching and learning needs. People began viewing their computers and gadgets as tools for fun rather than seeing them as unique learning opportunities that could help unlock every student's potential.

While I may not have been able to ultimately get Apple management's support for implementing the ideas in our book, I was fortunate that its message spread rapidly across the world, from Mexico to the UK, to Japan, Korea, and China. It was translated into multiple languages and within weeks had garnered critical acclaim, received all 5-star reviews on Amazon, and sold tens of thousands of copies. It was inspiring to see that the ideas Steve and I had discussed privately for so many years were finally gaining a mainstream audience. In China, *Rewiring Education* did so well that it ended up as the best-selling education book of 2019, showing that the demand for change was global.

I had now successfully added a new dot in my life and going forward I was free to do things in my own ways, on my own terms. Even though I was effectively pushed out of this *different* Apple, no one could ever take from me the decades of blood, sweat and tears that I put into the Apple that Steve built. I will forever be Apple's 54th employee, its first VP of Software, one of its proudest "Fathers of Lisa," its first VP of Education and, most importantly, a colleague and friend of one of the most legendary visionaries the world had ever known. It was a chaotic and extraordinary ride but that was my life at Apple and the Steve I knew.

AN INFINITE GAME

*"Let's go invent tomorrow rather than
worry about what happened yesterday."*

—STEVE JOBS

Several years prior to my leaving Apple, I had invited best-selling author Simon Sinek to join me and my education team in a presentation we were scheduled to give at an Apple international education conference. Simon's book, *Start with Why*, had inspired leaders all over the world to reassess the reason their companies and organizations existed, and challenged them to ask *Why* questions before even considering *What* and *How* questions. After our presentations Simon and I shared a taxi ride back to the airport. Along the way, we struck up an interesting conversation that touched on the differences between Apple and Microsoft's education philosophies that years later he would recall as part of a story in his next book, *The Infinite Game*.

   During our taxi ride, Simon told me that not long ago he had given a presentation at a Microsoft education conference and, now that he had done the same at Apple, he was intrigued by how differently education was viewed by the two companies. At Microsoft's presentation, Simon recalled, the executives got on stage and talked almost exclusively about "beating Apple." In contrast, he observed that every Apple presenter had spent

100 percent of their time talking about how Apple was trying to help teachers teach and students learn. His point was that, whereas Microsoft obsessed about beating its competition, Apple obsessed about advancing our *vision* for education or, as Simon called it, our "Just Cause."

As part of Simon's story on our discussion in *The Infinite Game*, he recalled telling me that Microsoft had given him a Zune portable music player and how he felt it was a better product than Apple's iPod. In my response to that, he quoted me as saying simply, "I have no doubt." I said that because I knew that a company supposedly having a "better" product meant little unless it properly reflected the organization's *Why* and Just Cause. I didn't care if people thought a Zune was better than an iPod (it wasn't), because individual products do not matter if their existence isn't a part of a bigger, long-term plan.

Let me share an example of what I mean by this. Apple's original iPod (2001) ultimately led to the iPhone (2004), which led to the iPod Touch (2007), which led to the iPad (2010), all powerful products, on a common integrated platform, with a wide ecosystem of apps that are, in turn, transforming teaching and learning all over the world. Did the Zune do that? OK, in fairness to Microsoft, they did release a follow-up product called the Zune HD, which lived for three whole years before the company killed the entire line of products for good. What the difference really boiled down to was company leadership and the things that they prioritized. Steve had what Simon refers to as "infinite vision" and instilled an urgent sense of purpose in everyone one of us who worked for him, which in turn made the products we developed purposeful as well.

At the end of Simon's story, he referred to my four-word response as being one "consistent with that of a leader with an *infinite mindset*." The term refers to a mentality that encourages leaders to actively initiate disruptive strategies or business models in order to advance progress in their Just Cause. In 2019, when I first read the book, I was honored to have been a part of such an influential work on leadership and, even more so, that he had such respect for my leadership. To be honest, Simon's entire book was inspiring, making me more determined than ever to not let anything get in my way of rewiring education—not even a global pandemic.

THE CORONA CALAMITY

In early 2020, much of the world was caught off-guard by the rapid spread and lethality of one of the worst global pandemics in history—Covid-19, more commonly referred to by the general public as the "coronavirus." While most adults had lived through at least one pandemic, never before had one spread around the world so quickly that it forced nearly every country to simultaneously take drastic measures to slow its spread. In the United States, a rare national emergency was declared at the federal level. This prompted most state governors to issue "stay-at-home orders," meaning that virtually everyone in the country, with the exception of "essential workers," were not allowed to leave their house. Almost overnight, every K-12 school in the country shut down halfway through the school year as parents, students, and teachers (controversially *not* classified as essential workers) found themselves on lockdown.

Prior to the coronavirus, most local governments and school districts had long been reluctant to invest in any significant technological resources. Rather than recognizing and utilizing its enormous potential, they stubbornly clung to Industrial Revolution education methods. Apparently, in order for students to learn, school administrators and education leaders believed that children needed to sit in traditional desks, in traditional classrooms, and be taught by traditional teachers in traditional ways. These misinformed beliefs continued even though vast numbers of students struggled to learn under such an outdated model.

But now, those same leaders found themselves in the midst of a rude awakening as the coronavirus was sounding alarms that they assumed they would never hear. School leaders had now found themselves watching helplessly as their traditional educational models buckled under pressure. Unfortunately, most of them chose not to invest in digital environments that would have allowed for an easy transition to remote learning and they had no viable backup plan. Various types of digital, homeschool, and remote learning models had existed long before the pandemic. None of them were perfect and many were highly affordable, some even free. The main reason school leaders didn't use them to supplement in-person learning wasn't because they were flawed or expensive, it was because they didn't think they *needed* them.

As it turned out, they were wrong. Suddenly, millions of principals, teachers, and parents were scrambling to figure out how to effectively use technology for remote learning. Educational software and hardware sales soared and most of them failed to deliver, due primarily to the lack of teacher training that's absolutely essential in making them work. To call what happened a *calamity* may be the biggest understatement in this book! Not only did school and district leaders significantly underestimate the need for remote models, digital curriculums, and teacher training, they never really had a new vision for the future of education.

Comparatively, Steve's vision for the future of education was *always* clear. As he so eloquently put it, "All books, learning materials, and assessments should be digital, interactive, tailored to each student, and provide feedback in real time." This was the kind of "infinite vision" that school leaders needed, prior to the lockdowns, in order to have prevented the complete shutdown of America's education system. It was unfortunate that they saw this only in hindsight, having ignored decades of visionary foresight.

JUST CAUSE

Steve's goal at Apple was never to just sell products, but to also sell the "why" behind those products. If we did it right, he would tell us, the products would sell themselves. As Vice President of Education, I had taken that philosophy to heart, which is why Simon heard me give that kind of passionate presentation at the conference. The "Just Cause" that powered Apple Education, during my tenure, was that we would always use products "as a means for transforming education to better meet the needs of today's digital natives." This was not a new concept, but it was a clear extension of Steve's very well-defined vision for education.

Unfortunately, by 2018 Apple began to shift away from its educational Just Cause and more toward traditional sales models. This was reflected in key decisions made that included: disbursing the education division across the company, ignoring the findings of their own $ACOT^2$ research and its challenge-based learning solutions, and abandoning iTunes U, a platform that had the potential to become the digital distribution channel for personalized learning during the coronavirus attack. These changes altered the philosophy that Apple Education had operated under for the previous eighteen years—with students ultimately paying the price.

EDUCATION REWIRED

The success of *Rewiring Education* has shown me just how many people want real educational change. On nearly a daily basis I hear from people who believe as strongly as I do that the purpose of education should not be just memorization, but to help children discover their unique genius and empower them to reach beyond all perceived limitations. While technology by itself will never be able to solve as complex a puzzle as education, there is no doubt that going forward it will, and *must*, play a significant role. Innovative technologies like smart phones and watches, apps, social and interactive media, and artificial intelligence have come to successfully supplement nearly every modern industry and are continuously being integrated into nearly every aspect of our lives, rewiring our homes, jobs, cars, and even our brains! Everything, that is, *except* education. This *must* change.

After retiring from Apple, I was ready to start adding new, exciting dots in my life. The difference this time around, however, was that I would look to *intentionally* connect them with my past experiences, just as Steve had suggested during his Stanford commencement speech. I used to be a look-forward-only kind of guy, but I've now come to understand that it's impossible to get where I want to go without understanding and appreciating where I've been. By relying on lessons learned from programs and experiences like Kids Can't Wait, ACOT and ACOT², Santa Fe Christian Academy, iTunes, and ConnectEd, I began my post-Apple endeavors by actively looking for opportunities to rewire education. Within just the first couple of years after leaving Apple, I was off and running by leading, funding, or otherwise supporting several entities, including three highly ambitious ventures: Beyond Schools, Oxford Day Academy, and an online, fully accredited professional development university.

Beyond Schools is a digital, online challenge-based learning curriculum for kids ages three through sixteen, ingeniously created by Knotion, an award-winning educational software developer in Mexico. It's my intent to make their digital curriculum freely available to individual students as they bring their product to U.S. schools. Oxford Day Academy (ODA) is a lab school headed by Mallory Dwinell, a talented, Harvard-educated leader, who has successfully integrated the Oxford tutorial method and the CBL pedagogy, allowing students to spend as much time working outside of school as they do inside classrooms. ODA has had exceptional success, by any measure, even though it caters specifically to disadvantaged high school students who come in three- to four-grade levels behind. Finally, I helped fund an accredited online school, called Reach University, designed to train teachers how to use proven, but underutilized pedagogies, like challenge-based learning and the Oxford tutorial method. The program will work in conjunction with a unique teacher internship program that trains rural educators in twenty-first-century teaching and learning methods and will actively work to help end the national teacher shortage.

I will do everything I can to help rewire education for the rest of my life. I will also continue doing everything I can to provide the opportunity for *all* students to have equal access to effective digital resources and individualized remote learning. Last but not least, I will continue trying to ensure that every teacher has access to the professional development they need to properly prepare students for the challenges of today and tomorrow. As optimistic a person as I am, I'm also a realist, and I know that accomplishing such lofty goals will be incredibly challenging. I understand that it can't be done alone, which is why I'm committed to surrounding myself with like-minded people, empowered by infinite mindsets, and always thinking different, just like the nuts on top of Steve's Apple sundae.

ONE MORE THING. . .

In *The Infinite Game*, Simon Sinek notes that visionary leaders often create major disruptions that appear to the outside world as though they can predict the future. "They can't," he assures us. "They do, however, operate with a clear and fixed vision of a future state that does not yet exist—their Just Cause—and constantly scan for ideas, opportunities or technologies that can help them advance toward that vision." In other words, *Steve Jobs*.

Steve's perceived ability to predict the future was actually his single-minded obsession to *invent* it. Unlike many leaders in education today, he believed in being proactive rather than reactive, and always preferred innovation over tradition. For generations finite leadership has failed education, steadily devolving our schools into what has become little more than a sea of standardized tests, giving students and parents a false sense of future success.

Education is an *infinite* game and there is no end to infinite games. This game has nothing to do with designing the best computer or with who sells the most. Nothing to do with a student's ability to learn something by some arbitrary date. Nothing to do with letter grades, test scores, or GPAs. No, the primary objective of education's infinite game isn't to win, but to continue playing for as long as possible, looking backward to connect dots that will forever push us forward. That's the game the Steve I knew taught me how to play and the one I will continue to play well beyond my life at Apple.

ACKNOWLEDGMENTS

I originally attempted to capture Apple's uniqueness in 1984 with a manuscript titled *Leadership by Vision,* but I put it aside because I wanted to test its concepts in the education market. The manuscript was dedicated to four individuals whose vision, leadership and commitment to "what can be" changed my life. It now seems fitting to resurrect that dedication, 36 years later, as their wisdom and influence remains true today. Thus, it is my distinct honor to dedicate this book:

To Steve Jobs: In his memory, the pirate, visionary, dreamer and motivator who knew no fear or boundaries and always challenged me to do the impossible. I dedicate this book to you because I shared your vision and because you showed me the *way* to change the world.

To Mike (ACM) Markkula: A true professional, thinker and tinkerer who understood the real meaning of leadership and who always encouraged me with genuine caring and support. I dedicate this book to you because of the respect I have for your personal leadership and because you showed me *how* to change the world.

To Stan Johnson: Pastor, sage and guide, who lived a life of humbleness, sincerity and service, and who taught me the strength and power of faith. I dedicate this book to you because you showed me *why* I need to change the world.

To Steve (Woz) Wozniak: The engineering genius and close friend whose kindness and compassion is always contagious. I dedicate this book to you because your humility and brilliance taught me *what* would change the world.

Finally, to my dedicated Apple team for 21 years: the workers, creators, innovators, geniuses, philosophers, stargazers, heroes, artists, thinkers and designers who took risky and unknown steps with me on a journey that *did* change the world.

—John Dennis Couch